Boxing Plato's Shadow

An Introduction to the Study of Human Communication

MICHAEL DUES
MARY BROWN

University of Arizona

McGraw-Hill Higher Education

A Division of The McGraw-Hill Companies

Boxing PLATO'S SHADOW
An Introduction to the Study of Human Communication

567890   QSR QSR   0987654

ISBN 0-07-250861-2

Editor: Nada Mraovic
Cover Design: Maggie Lytle
Printer/Binder: Quebecor World

Contents

---

dedicated to Robert Gunderson

Foreword to Instructors

This book is about the systematic study of communication over its 2500-year history, and about opportunities to apply the knowledge produced by this study to achieve better communication outcomes. Those who seek to become professional scholars, teachers, or practitioners of communication should have a basic understanding of the origins of our ideas about communication, the key issues with which communication scholars struggle, and the processes by which knowledge about communication is generated. In this introduction to our field we hope to provide a starting point for this understanding.

This work is neither a complete history of the discipline nor an exhaustive description of contemporary approaches to communication study. Rather, it is a brief overview whose purpose is to orient newcomers to this centrally important and always fascinating field of study. It summarizes the rhetorical and social scientific roots of communication study, the contemporary methods employed to advance our understanding of human communication, and challenges and opportunities facing communication students, scholars and professionals. Throughout, it emphasizes the field's durability over more than two millennia and the merits of multiple systematic approaches to the study of communication.

As others have aptly pointed out, histories are by nature reconstructed and rhetorical. This little volume is no exception. Attempting to tell a balanced, concise story of our field is a humbling experience. Our challenge is to tell a big story in a small book. In striving for brevity and coherence, we surely err in leaving some gaps, and in giving the impression of greater continuity of events than what actually occurred. Moreover, our own personal experiences as communication scholars and practitioners prompted us to write from a particular point of view; one that is based on a deep appreciation for the classical roots and the contemporary possibilities of this special field.

M.D. and M.B.

Note to Student Readers

This book is an introduction to the study of communication for students and others new to our field. Its purpose is to give you the background to see where you fit in to our field, and to equip you to participate in the practice of communication study. It tells about how the field came to be what it is. It tells about what communication scholars and practitioners do and have done for more than two millennia. It asks you to consider where you fit in, and what your interests are. You will stand on the shoulders of scholars who have gone before you. You have the opportunity to see farther than they have—you can see from today's broad perspective.

Those of you who complete degrees at the bachelors or masters level will be equipped to be practitioners of the art of communication, in your personal life, your community life, and your professional occupations. It's important to remember how old and broad your professional and intellectual roots are as you proceed in your personal and professional endeavors.

Some of you will go on to advanced study and will carry on the research in our field. Our hope is that you will appreciate the many streams of ideas that come together in the study of communication, and that you will see the merits of blending the many ways of studying the subject. Finally, we hope that you will work side-by-side with those of different background and worldviews so that you can enrich and challenge each other to reach greater understanding of this exceptional field.

M.D. and M.B.

Introduction

Studying Communication

Robert Gunderson, a venerable communication scholar and teacher, once described communication study as a "discipline of refugees." He observed that many communication scholars began their careers intending to be something else—psychologists, sociologists, literary critics, or historians. Like Dr. Gunderson, we find it ironic that communication is a second choice of subjects for so many scholars, for it would be hard to find a human activity more ubiquitous and more essential than communicating. Research studies tell us that about 75 percent of the average person's day is engaged in some form of communication. One estimate suggests that "we listen a book a day, speak a book a week, read the equivalent of a book a month, and write the equivalent of a book a year (Buckley, 1992). Communication is a primary means of meeting our needs and accomplishing our goals. We communicate to share information, ideas, and feelings; to influence one another; to co-ordinate activity; to build relationships; to acquire goods and services; to entertain and express ourselves; and to create and sustain the cultures that enable us to prosper in civilized communities. Another way of saying "humans are *social* animals" is to say "humans are *communicating* animals."

How *well* we communicate matters, probably more than how *much*. Individuals, organizations, and communities who communicate effectively have an evolutionary advantage over those who fail to communicate as well; they get better results. That is why communication skills are listed as primary in virtually every contemporary study of job skills (Daily, 1999; Floyd & Gordon, 1998), and why they are recognized as critical in job roles ranging from entry-level positions to executive officers. It's not surprising, then, that when 1000 college faculty members from a variety of academic disciplines were asked what skills every college graduate would need, they placed communication at the very top of the list (Morreale & Vogl, 1998). Better communication helps us to succeed and prosper in our enterprises and in our personal relationships. And better understanding of the processes and functions of communication enables us to communicate more effectively.

Given the crucial link between better communication and a better life, communication has been a subject of serious study in many cultures, throughout recorded history. The first book on this subject is almost as old as writing itself. Around 2675 BC, an Egyptian named Ptah Hotep offered advice on communication in a book called *Precepts*, which he used in his role as instructor to the Pharoah's sons (Reinard, 1998). His book served for centuries as a textbook for Egyptians. In the *Bible*, Jesus teaches an important lesson about communication through the parable of the "sewer of seeds", suggesting that while it is the speaker's responsibility to state the truth, it is up to the hearer to receive and heed it (Peters, 1999). The *Koran* clearly addresses human communication, instructing people to make their messages true and straightforward (Ali, 1996). In ancient China, advice on effective, appropriate communication could be found in the Lao-Tzu. In the early fifteenth century, Seami, a Japanese author, advised that the ultimate goal of discourse "lies in a grace of language and complete mastery of the speech of the nobility and gentry, so that even the most casual utterance will be graceful" (Zeuschner, 1997).

Today the study of human communication is an important academic discipline that investigates the ways people relate to and affect one another through the messages they send and receive. It is a thriving and growing enterprise, encompassing thousands of scholars, and research on every aspect of human communication from the most intimate interpersonal interactions to the broadest effects of mass media. Professional associations of communication scholars have formed at the international, national, regional, and state levels. At annual conferences members of these associations gather to share and discuss their findings. More than 30 academic journals focus on communication research. What we learn from this research builds the knowledge base for educating students and training professionals across multiple disciplines.

In the midst of this thriving academic and professional activity there exists an intriguing paradox. Despite the centrality of communication among human behaviors, the long history of communication study in Western Civilization, and the vitality of communication research today, the discipline faces a continuing struggle for recognition as a legitimate academic pursuit separate from other disciplines. And, despite the obvious importance of communication in accomplishing organizational and community objectives, communication specialists often face a similar struggle for recognition of their substantial contributions to organizational goals.

This recognition problem is partly due to the fact that while communication has been studied and taught for 2,500 years, the focus of communication study and its name have shifted over time. From the time of the ancient Greeks until the eighteenth century, the study of communication focused primarily on the art of persuading others through speech, and was called *rhetoric*. During the nineteenth century Europeans and Americans sought to build their ability to speak gracefully and effectively by studying what they called *elocution*, emphasizing voice, diction, and gesture. In the early twentieth century teachers of public speaking sought to distinguish their discipline from English by focusing on spoken communication and calling their discipline *speech*. The word *communication*, as we understand and use it today, was introduced into English vocabulary by John Locke in 1690 (Peters, 1999), but use of this term to name our discipline did not become common until about 1960. Thus, while our discipline has a long history and deep roots in western civilization, it has evolved slowly, traveled under a variety of labels, and only recently acquired its name. We can understand, then, why communication is perceived by some as a new discipline, one that has yet to clearly delineate its subject matter and boundaries.

A second reason communication must struggle for recognition is that we study a *process* that cuts across many other disciplines. Aspects of the communication process are studied by anthropologists, sociologists, historians, political scientists, theologians, clinical and social psychologists, health educators, and organizational theorists. Within their fields, these scholars study communication under such subject areas as sociolinguistics, homiletics, marital interaction, and public relations, just to name a few. Because it is a ubiquitous, on-going process that is integral to human interaction, communication is difficult to define in simple terms separate from the subject matter of other disciplines.

A third reason why the study of communication may be viewed as having dubious value is that humans can use it as a means to deceive and exploit one another just as surely as they can use it to share truth and build community. It was this susceptibility to misuse that led Plato to argue forcefully against the teaching of rhetoric in ancient Athens, and that often leads us to doubt the words of press secretaries or the integrity of attorneys today. Whatever the reasons, our enterprise is viewed as marginal by many scholars and professionals (Taylor, 1999). Thus, sooner or later all communication scholars confront the necessity not only to explain their discipline, but also to defend it.

One result of this paradoxical problem is that many scholars have taken up communication as a second or third career choice. In describing communication study as a discipline of refugees Robert Gunderson spoke from the experience. Over the course of his career he guided 49 graduate students to their doctoral degrees (Ritter, 2001). "We came to this study," he said, "because there were important questions to answer about communication that we couldn't address adequately in our home disciplines" (R. G. Gunderson, personal communication, 1968). Dr. Gunderson was talking about professional scholars more than thirty years ago, but a similar phenomenon occurs today when college students choose their major. Many of our students immigrate to our discipline when they discover that by studying communication they can gain highly relevant knowledge and skills which they could not acquire in their original majors. Once engaged, they quickly see that communication is central to human interaction, that greater competence in communication means greater ability to meet our own, our family's, and our community's needs, and that improved communication can mean improved quality of life. Robert Gunderson's key point was that the discipline of communication enables us to answer critically important questions about human communication and how we can improve it— questions that are not as effectively addressed in any other discipline.

If you are a newcomer to our discipline, we welcome you. You are entering a worthwhile and fascinating field of endeavor. In the chapters that follow, we offer a basic orientation to the academic and professional discipline of communication by addressing several key questions:

- What are our roots as a discipline? Where did this study come from? How did it arrive at its current status? Why is a subject so central and important so under-recognized and misunderstood?

- What are some of the fundamental concepts that guide our efforts to understand and improve human communication?

- What methods do scholars employ to produce new knowledge about human communication? What kinds of things do communication scholars study?

Today we study communication as a central force in contemporary life, but our concept of communication has evolved as an outcome of 2500 years of thought, study, and practice. It is an idea we have *inherited*, shaped over the centuries by changing political and social conditions, and by technological advances. To appreciate and fully comprehend the study of human communication, one must know the story of how it came to be what it is. That story begins in ancient Athens with a very practical problem and a group of teachers known as sophists.

References

Ali, S. S. (1996, Summer). Foundation for communication in the Qur'an and Sunnah. *The American Journal of Islamic Social Sciences*, 13(2), 225-245.

Buckley, M.H. (1992, December). Focus on research: We listen a book a book a day; speak a book a week: Learning from Walter Loban. *Language Arts*, 69, 623.

Daily, J. A. (1999, January). Communication matters. *Spectra*, 35(1), 2,12-14.

Floyd C. J. & Gordon M. E. (1998, Summer). What skills are most important? A comparison of employer, student and staff perceptions. *Journal of Marketing Education*, 20(2), 103-110.

Morreale, S. P. & Vogl, M. W. (1998). *Pathways to careers in communication*. Annandale, VA: National Communication Association.

Peters, J. D. (1999). *Speaking into the air: A history of the idea of communication*. Chicago: University of Chicago Press.

Reinard, J. C. (1998). The role of research in communication. In *Introduction to communication research* (2nd ed.) (pp. 2-25). Boston: McGraw-Hill.

Ritter, K. (2001). Robert Gray Gunderson: The historian as civic rhetorician. In J. A. Kuypers & A. King (Eds.), *Twentieth-century roots of rhetorical studies* (pp. 175-209). Westport, CT: Preager Publishers.

Taylor, O. L., (1999, April). What is the discipline of communication? *Spectra*, 33(4), 2, 12.

Zeuchner, R. (1997). *Communicating today* (2nd ed.). Boston: Allyn and Bacon.

Chapter 1

The Beginning of Communication Study

Athens reached the peak of its economic and military prominence during the fifth century B.C. Arguably the strongest and wealthiest of Greek city states, Athens had merchant ships trading throughout the Mediterranean basin, a great navy, a powerful army, magnificent structures and beautiful art. The great Athenian legacy that concerns us here, however, resulted not from the city's power or its beauty, but from two important innovations in its governance: the adversary system of justice, and democracy. These two developments gave advantages to citizens who could communicate effectively, and thus led to the study of communication.

The Adversary System was invented by the Greeks as an alternative to fighting among themselves. The basic premise of this system was that when two citizens found themselves in a dispute over property or some perceived offense, they would agree in advance to let a respected third party serve as judge. Each of the disputing parties would argue his case before the judge who, based upon his evaluation of the merits of their arguments, would decide how the dispute should be settled. In settling conflicts among citizens, this approach amounted to replacing physical combat, which was painful and dangerous, with verbal combat, which was an obvious improvement. Over time this approach was formalized into a court system, and extended to apply to judging the

1

guilt or innocence of persons accused of crimes. Although in subsequent centuries various states have added and improved details, the adversary system remains the best available judicial process.

Democracy was adopted as a replacement for tyranny in Athens during the sixth century BC. Tyranny is the form of governance in which a single ruler has absolute, unquestioned authority over every-thing. With a wise and beneficent ruler tyranny can be tolerable; with a bad tyrant it is terribly oppressive. So, under the leadership of Solon and Cleisthenes, Athens instituted reforms, adopting a system of gov-ernment in which citizens assembled and made decisions by majority vote. Thereafter, the Athenian Assembly debated and decided by voting on such matters as official appointments, laws, declaring war, or ac-cepting a proposed peace treaty. This was democracy in an embryonic form. Only a small minority of the Athenian population—male citi-zens—participated. Women were forbidden to speak publicly, or to vote. Non-citizen merchants, traders, professionals, and ambassadors were excluded, as were slaves. Still, the ancient Athenians invented, and successfully applied, the basic method of democratic governance.

A MARKET FOR COMMUNICATION KNOWLEDGE AND SKILL

In Athenian courts citizens were required to advocate cases for them-selves; and citizens spoke for themselves in the Assembly. The ability to speak persuasively was thus a skill that one needed to function as an Athenian citizen. Moreover, people who were more skilled in speaking than others had an obvious advantage. They won court cases and thus acquired more wealth; they also acquired position, status, and power by being impressive and influential in the Assembly. Success in public speaking became a means to greater wealth, status, and power. As Athenian citizens sought to improve their speaking ability, they created an obvious market for knowledge and skills in public speaking. Since these skills had monetary and status value, Athenians were willing to pay for them.

THE SOPHISTS

The systematic study of communication began in Athens during the 5th century BC in response to this market. Persons who studied and taught persuasive public speaking were known as *sophists*. They called this subject *rhetoric*. The term "sophist" had been used in Athens since the sixth century BC to refer to learned men, wise men, poets, and teachers (Barrett, 1987). Most sophists charged fees for their services.

Most early sophists were foreigners in Athens, ambassadors or traveling teachers from other cities. They taught a broad range of subjects in addition to rhetoric, offering a curriculum "designed to teach the Greek ideal of *arete:* the knowledge and attitude of effective participation in domestic, social, and political life" (Barrett, 1987). Sophists believed that all reasonably intelligent persons could become knowledgeable and acquire the skills to speak well—a view that offended some older, more traditional and elitist Athenians who clung to the belief that one's destiny was predetermined at birth. It is important to remember that in their study and teaching of rhetoric, sophists focused primarily on *public* speaking, which occurred primarily in the Assembly or the court, and in which only male Athenian citizens were permitted to engage. Focusing on skills for which there was a market, they addressed only one aspect of the broad subject of communication, and they served only a privileged few. Still, they launched the study of rhetoric and originated some of our most fundamental concepts of communication.

Several sophists contributed particularly important insights about rhetoric that have endured, and continue to influence the study and practice of communication.

Corax (who may be a legendary or composite figure) is generally credited with inventing the study of rhetoric, with identifying the different parts of a speech, and with defining the concept of "probability." Corax recognized that there are many matters about which we cannot be certain, but about which we can make rational judgments concerning what is most probably true. He thus provided a basis for treating argument and persuasion not merely as ways of advocating what we believe to be *certainly* true, but also as ways of discovering what is *probably* true (Cohen, 1994).

Protagoras built upon the concept of probability, and contributed the important idea that there are two sides to every argument. Protagoras suggested that the "truth" of one side should be tested by the "truth" of the other, and that advocates for each side have the burden of proving their side stronger (Barrett, 1987). For his contribution, Protagoras is credited with being the "father of debate" (Cohen, 1994).

Gorgias showed that public speeches could excite and inspire people. Admired for his beautiful style in the use of language, he focused on oratory that bordered on poetry, and taught that through great oratory one could "stop fear and banish grief and create joy and nurture piety" (Barrett, 1987, p. 15). Gorgias also appears to have developed the concept of *kairos*, which states that a speaker should adapt his oratory to suit the audience and the occasion (Barrett, 1987).

Hippias advocated that speakers must be broadly knowledgeable, able to answer all questions about a subject. He taught that it was necessary to keep acquiring new knowledge throughout one's life, and focused on ways to remember what one learned so that knowledge could be used to answer questions and build arguments (Cohen, 1994). In a famous debate with Socrates, Hippias argued that it was important to always have new things to say on a subject, while Socrates countered that truth was eternal, and that it was more important to speak the same enduring truths consistently (Barrett, 1987).

During the 4th century B.C., *Isocrates* brought together much of the teaching of fifth century B.C. sophists. An important teacher of rhetoric, he is thought to have significantly influenced the rhetorical thought of Aristotle, Cicero, and Quintilian (Kennedy, 1963).

Taken together, the sophists not only began the systematic study of communication, but also brought about major advances in Greek thought. They challenged the older Athenian beliefs that human lives were predetermined re-enactments of archetypal events that had already occurred among the gods. They advocated the revolutionary idea that humans are decision-making creatures who can affect their own environment and their personal and community fortunes, and who can influence one another by communicating effectively. They proposed that probable truth can be pursued by testing ideas in debate. They advanced the profoundly democratic idea that *every citizen* can *and should* learn to speak well and become influential (Barrett, 1987). And they taught that developing the skills and knowledge needed for citizenship was the duty of each citizen. The fundamental concepts and skills provided by the sophists made democracy possible. The practical study of "rhetoric" which they developed became a central subject in education curricula, and remained so for more than 2,000 years.

Given the important contributions made by the sophists to the development of Greek thought, to Western Civilization, and to the study of human communication, it seems oddly paradoxical that they and their subject are held today in such low esteem. This paradox is at least somewhat understandable when we consider that skill in communication in general, and persuasion in particular can be used deceive as well as to inform. In every era of history, there have been persons who deceive and manipulate others through communication. Con artists and demagogues make a point of becoming effective persuaders, using every known rhetorical device to achieve their ends. So, for many people, being persuaded becomes associated with being fooled, misled, deceived, or defrauded.

In ancient Athens, some sophists were less ethical than those we discussed above. Some went so far as to claim that truth did not matter, only effective persuasive technique. The reputations of the sophists, and of the study of rhetoric suffered accordingly. But the facts that communication can be used for either good or ill, and that some sophists were unethical, do not fully explain the negative public image still carried by rhetoric in particular, and by the study of communication in general. The influence of the great philosopher, Plato, is a significant additional factor.

PLATO'S SHADOW

To understand Plato's hostility toward the sophists and their work, we need to know about conditions in Athens in Plato's time. During the fifth century BC, military and economic success changed Athens from a close-knit city-state whose citizens shared coherent beliefs and values, into a cosmopolitan metropolis populated by diverse people who spoke different languages, held varying beliefs, and practiced a wide variety of customs. Foreigners brought to Athens attractive new ideas and goods, many of which challenged old Athenian ideas and customs. Many Athenians viewed these changes as corruptions of their pure beliefs and values; they longed for, and advocated returning to, Athens' older values and simpler ways. When Athens began to lose battles and wealth during the 4th century BC, these conservatives attributed their city's decline to its straying from traditional values under the influence of foreigners. Sophists who offered new ideas were controversial in Athens because they were seen by many as subverting traditional Athenian beliefs (Barrett, 1987).

Socrates was an important and unsettling voice. He challenged not traditional Athenian beliefs, but the newer ideas and mores associated with democratic governance that had taken hold in the fifth century BC (Smith, 1998). Uncomfortable with governance by a majority of ordinary men who were not particularly learned or wise, he sought to limit movement toward expanded democracy. He was suspicious of attempts by people to persuade one another, which formed the basis of the new democratic process. Believing that humans are to seek Truth by going inside themselves, he sought to help individuals discover truth not by persuading them, but only by asking questions during dialogues.

Socrates rarely made speeches or presented arguments; rather, he professed to know very little. He preferred and taught a more interactive way of communicating, asking challenging questions which provoked deeper thought on the part of his hearers. His method of drawing out, or "educing" truths from his students, is still applied; we call it the "Socratic method" today. And the Greek word "educe," which means to draw out, is the root of our word, "education."

Socrates preferred to think of communication as a profound, intimate enacting of relationship between two persons. He objected to the use of writing because the writer could not control who would read his message, nor when or where it would be read. Compared to his ideal of intimate communication, Socrates viewed rhetoric as, at best, a base pursuit (Peters, 1999).

Socrates' most influential follower was Plato. Plato opposed democracy on the fundamental grounds that truth is fixed and should be sought only by philosophers. A central point in his great work, *The Republic*, is that the best government would be one in which the best philosopher rules as king. Plato was uncomfortable with the idea that ordinary citizens should presume to advocate or to participate in governmental decision-making (Kennedy, 1963; Smith, 1998).

In keeping with his views on truth and democracy, Plato viewed the sophists and their ideas as harmful influences in Athens, and sought to discredit them. He did not distinguish between good and bad sophists; he painted them all with the same dark brush. He objected to the study of rhetoric on the grounds that rhetoricians favored style over substance and valued technique more than truth. The best he could say for rhetoric was that it might be seen as a utilitarian craft, about equal to cookery in difficulty or complexity, that might be used by philosophers to explain truths to ordinary citizens (Kennedy, 1963; Plato, 370BC/1937).

Plato advocated pursuit of universal Truth, and he cast Socrates in his written dialogues as the ethical inquirer in contrast to the unethical sophists (Smith, 1998). Plato's attacks on the sophists were somewhat self-serving, since he operated a school, charged fees for instruction, and was in direct competition with the sophists for students. It is also interesting to note that Plato used Socrates in his written dialogues as a potent *rhetorical device* to advance his persuasive arguments against rhetoric and the sophists-a strategy that enacted some of the very behaviors to which he was objecting. Nevertheless, Plato was so convincing in his attacks on rhetoric and the sophists that he succeeded in casting a permanent dark shadow over their reputations.

In later centuries, both Christian and Islamic scholars, who believed in divine inspiration, and who accepted the authority of scripture, would find Plato's view of rhetoric compatible with their beliefs. Divine truth for them was not debatable. In modern times, secular scholars, especially scientists, devoted to the ideal of achieving certainty through disciplined systematic research would identify with Plato's insistence on pursuit of certain truth. For them, the messy vagaries of rhetoric would epitomize the kind of thinking science was invented to overcome. Thus, over time, both religious and scientifically-minded scholars have shared Plato's low opinion of rhetoric.

ARISTOTLE'S RESOLUTION

Aristotle was Plato's leading student. Aristotle studied, taught, and wrote about literally every subject known to the ancient Greeks. He saw merit in both Plato's and the sophists' positions concerning the study of rhetoric, and applied himself to discovering ways to reconcile the two opposing views (Aristotle, 350BC/1991). While he respected and admired Plato, and served as an instructor in Plato's school, Aristotle differed with his great mentor on several key issues.

While Plato sought Truth as a philosopher, using reasoning and dialogue to "draw out" knowledge and understanding, Aristotle sought to understand his natural and social environment as a scientist would, by systematically observing. He has been called the first true empiricist because he practiced systematic observation, using the senses, then applied logic to his observations to form conclusions about nature, and about people. For Socrates and Plato, Truth resided within the person, and was to be discovered by being drawn out. For Aristotle, Truth was all around in the environment, and was to be taken in through the senses.

For matters concerning which certainty was attainable, Aristotle sided with Socrates and Plato in advocating the use of dialectic, the art of arriving at truth through philosophical disputation. For use in dialectic, Aristotle invented *formal logic*. Perhaps Aristotle's greatest contribution to civilization, logic served to guide thoughts to sure conclusions. It consisted of *syllogisms*, in which specific claims based on observation were combined with known universal principles to draw conclusions. While Plato's devotion to pursuit of truth provided the ideal for academic scholarship, Aristotle's empirical perspective and system of logic provided the fundamental methods for pursuing that ideal.

The key point on which Aristotle differed from Plato and agreed with Isocrates was his observation that on many issues humans could at best ascertain only "probable" truth. He recognized that most decisions in matters of state rested not on certainties but on these relative probabilities. Important decisions were made on the basis of judgments about what was probable (Aristotle, 350BC/1991). On matters where only probable truth could be ascertained, Aristotle recognized persuasion and advocacy, the tools of the sophists' trade, as valid decision making tools. He observed that persuasive advocacy in fact influenced decisions in both the courts and the Assembly. Agreeing with Protagoras, he reasoned that on matters where certainty could not be reached, advocacy and debate were the best available means of discovering what was most probably true (Aristotle, 350BC/1991).

Based on his observations, Aristotle also differed from his master about the ethics of studying and teaching rhetoric as a way to discover truth. Plato viewed rhetoric as suspect because it could be used to promote falsehood over truth, and thus steered honorable men away from it. Aristotle, on the other hand, saw that rhetoric could be used to promote either falsehood *or* truth, and he concluded that it was the *duty* of honorable citizens to arm themselves with knowledge and skill in rhetoric in order to defend truth (Aristotle, 350BC/1991). He reasoned that truth is naturally easier to defend than falsehood. Thus, he argued, if honorable men are well armed with rhetorical skills they should always be able to prevail over the advocates of falsehood. If good men fail to develop rhetorical skill, he said, they will have only themselves to blame when falsehood prevails (Aristotle, 350BC/1932).

Based on the above rationale, Aristotle studied and taught rhetoric. He drew upon many of the ideas of the sophists, added useful concepts of his own, and developed a complete system of rhetoric. Aristotle's system was laid out in his *Rhetoric*, which is recognized as the most complete of all ancient works on the subject, and which provides the starting point for most twentieth century study of persuasive communication. Aristotle defined "rhetoric" as "the art of discovering all the available means of persuasion in a given situation" (Aristotle, 350BC/1991). He carefully distinguished rhetoric from logic and dialectic, assigning each subject specific functions. Whereas logic employed the precise construction of *syllogisms*, Aristotle noted that rhetoric was accomplished through a somewhat looser form of reasoning, which he called the *emthymeme*. Enthymemes differed from strict syllogisms in two ways: (1) they relied premises that were generally, or probably true, rather than on premises that must be certainly and universally true; and (2) parts of the argument were often left unspoken, and filled in mentally by the audience.

Many of the basic concepts that frame and guide our contemporary study of human communication were articulated by Aristotle in the *Rhetoric*. These include the following:

- Communication is "purposive." That is, people communicate with the *intention* of affecting or influencing others, and communication efforts can be evaluated on the basis of whether they succeeded, if so, how, and if not, why not.

- Communication efforts (oratory) can be categorized by purpose and situation into three types: *forensic oratory* is speaking in the courts as an adversary; *deliberative oratory* is speaking in the assembly to influence a decision; *epideictic oratory* is speaking at a ceremony on a special occasion to inspire listeners.

- Persuasion is accomplished through a combination of three kinds of appeals:

  Ethos (Personal appeal of the speaker. Today we call this *source credibility*.)

  Logos (Logical support provided by the speaker. Today we call this *argument*.)

  Pathos (Emotional appeal, the stimulating of an emotional response in the audience.)

  In observing that persuasion is affected not only by reason, but also by the credibility of the speaker's character and emotions of the audience, Aristotle made it clear that persuasion is both a logical and a psychological process.

- Learning to speak effectively is a matter of developing five skills:

  Invention is the ability to generate the ideas needed to be persuasive in a given situation.

  Disposition is the ability to organize the ideas for maximum impact.

  Style is the ability to use language appropriately in any situation.

  Memory is the ability to remember facts and ideas.

  Delivery is the ability to speak in a clear, strong voice and with effective gestures.

  These skills were later employed by the great Roman teacher of rhetoric, Quintilian, to structure his instructions on rhetoric, and came to be known as the *"five canons of rhetoric"* (Clarke, 1953).

During Aristotle's lifetime Greece was conquered by the Macedonians. Drafted into the service of King Philip of Macedon, Aristotle was appointed to serve as teacher to Philip's son, Alexander. Aristotle exercised considerable influence on young Alexander, whom we now know as Alexander the Great. Alexander took copies of Aristotle's works along on his conquest of the then known world, and had them translated into Arabic and Persian languages. Almost two centuries later, when the Romans conquered Greece, they were eager to acquire Greek knowledge. Aristotle's *Rhetoric* and the writings of the sophists served as key sources of rhetorical understanding for Cicero, Rome's greatest orator and, later, for Quintilian, who taught rhetoric in Rome (Clarke, 1953). For most of the next two thousand years, rhetoric was treated as one of the fundamental arts that all educated persons were expected to know. Aristotle's *Rhetoric* inspired nineteenth century English rhetoricians, George Campbell, Richard Whately, and Hugh Blair (Smith, 1998). And, in twentieth century American universities, the *Rhetoric* became the cornerstone of the academic discipline of Speech Communication.

Aristotle provided a foundation for the study of human communication, but his work did not fully dispel the suspicions about rhetoric that Plato had raised. To this day the term " rhetoric" is often used to refer to hollow persuasive messages lacking substance and containing pretentious language. "Sophistry" is understood to mean specious argument, or the tricky use of style to deceive an audience. Sophists still are generally regarded as shallow thinkers and mercenaries who lacked a moral compass, in contrast to Socrates, who is viewed as the highly ethical martyr to his beliefs. Plato's negative portrayal of rhetoric and its teachers in his dialogue, *Gorgias*, still rings true for readers. Twenty-five hundred years later, the shadow Plato cast over the study of persuasive communication persists.

BOXING PLATO'S SHADOW

Communication's public relations problem has its roots in the excesses of some sophists, in Plato's strong objections to the study of rhetoric, and in the fact that communication can be used to deceive as well as to inform. A line in an old Woody Guthrie song says "Some rob you with a six gun, some with a fountain pen." In democracies, there will always be demagogues and crooked politicians who work at perfecting the art of the lie. Sharing their expertise in communication with such disreputable characters, communication practitioners and scholars may always be subject to suspicion. Despite this drawback, as authors and teachers, we support Aristotle's position that good people have a responsibility to learn the mechanisms of persuasion to ensure that truth will prevail. So we join other scholars in our field in promoting the responsible study of communication by honorable people. In doing so we take our place in the study of communication as a central aspect of education from ancient times to our own.

Years ago, as a young college professor, I (M. D.) spent a heated hour on a September afternoon arguing with a film instructor about the value of teaching students rhetorical sensitivity and skills. He said he disapproved of my teaching argumentation and coaching debate on ethical grounds. I defended my profession, but my arguments, which seemed so strong and clear to me, seemed not to move him at all. He, of course, cited Plato and Socrates, holding that truth must be "educed," or drawn out of students by asking challenging questions. I, on the other hand, cited Aristotle. Driving home that evening, thinking about the afternoon's discussion, it occurred to me that I had not been arguing with my contemporary colleague so much as I had been doing battle with the old shadow Plato had cast over the study of rhetoric. The image came to mind of shadow boxing—punching at thin air the way boxers do in practice, striking nothing because the opponent isn't really there. I felt that I had spent the afternoon boxing Plato's shadow. Ever since that day, when I am required to explain or defend my discipline, the image of boxing Plato's shadow comes to mind.

CONTRIBUTIONS OF PLATO AND SOCRATES TO THE STUDY OF COMMUNICATION

In highlighting their opposition to the teaching of rhetoric we should not overlook the significant contributions of Socrates and Plato to our understanding of human communication. Rhetoric, after all, is only one aspect of communication, and one unfortunate consequence of rhetoric's occupying a central place in education for so many centuries may have been that a broader and deeper understanding of communication was not more effectively pursued. From a twentieth-century perspective, John Durham Peters (1999) has pointed out that Socrates provided a significant addition to the idea of communication. He offered a valuable ideal in viewing communication as an act of intimate relationship and reciprocity, resulting in discovery and appreciation of truth and beauty. Socrates saw great value in communication aimed at simply sharing truth, without seeking personal gain. Plato also added greatly to our understanding of human communication by describing the limits of rhetoric's value and its potential for misuse. Even Plato's shadow is an important contribution; it reminds us that communication is a powerful tool that can be used for good or ill, and prods us to be ethical communicators.

References

Aristotle. (1932). *The rhetoric of Aristotle* (L. Cooper, Trans.). Englewood Cliffs, NJ: Prentice Hall. (Original work written about 350 B.C.)

Aristotle. (1991). *On rhetoric: A theory of civic discourse* (G. A. Kennedy, Trans.). New York: Oxford University Press. (Original work written about 350 B.C.)

Barrett, H. (1987). *The Sophists.* Novato, CA: Chandler & Sharp Publishers, Inc.

Clarke, M. L. (1953). *Rhetoric at Rome: A historical survey.* London, England: Cohen & West Ltd.

Cohen, H. (1994). *The history of speech communication: The emergence of a discipline.* Annandale, VA: Speech Communication Association.

Kennedy, G. (1963). *The art of persuasion in Greece.* Princeton, NJ: Princeton University Press.

Plato. (1937). The dialogues (B. Jowett, Trans.). New York: Random House. (Original work written about 370 B.C.)

Peters, John D. (1999). *Speaking into the air: A history of the idea of communication.* Chicago: University of Chicago Press.

Smith, C. R. (1998). *Rhetoric and human consciousness: A history.* Prospect Heights, IL: Waveland Press.

Chapter 2

Communication Study from Aristotle's Time to the 20th Century

In Chapter 1 we observed that communication study is a 2500-year old endeavor, begun in ancient Athens by the sophists who focused on the study of rhetoric. We noted that rhetoric represents only one aspect of human communication and that Socrates suggested what he regarded as a higher ideal of personal communication. Plato argued forcefully against the teaching of rhetoric, but Aristotle recognized rhetoric's value and developed the basic concepts that serve as foundations for our knowledge of the subject. In this chapter, we will very briefly sketch the history of communication study from Aristotle's time to the twenti-eth century. For most of that long span the study and teaching of com-munication focused almost exclusively on rhetoric. Over the centuries, however, historical events combined with advances in knowledge and technology to broaden as well as to sharpen the focus of communica-tion study.

Rhetoric in Egypt and Rome

PRESERVATION IN EGYPT

As he marched through Persia and Egypt Alexander the Great carried with him a veritable library of writings from Aristotle, Plato, the sophists, and other Greeks. Intending to rule his newly conquered empire from an entirely new capitol that would reflect the many cultures of all his subjects, Alexander began construction of the city of Alexandria in Egypt. Near the center of that city he ordered construction of a great library to house all the important Greek works as well as writings from Egypt, Persia, and other newly conquered states. He ordered that all these works be translated into Arabic so that all scholars in his new empire could learn from them.

Alexander did not live to see his city or his library completed. He became ill (some believe he was poisoned) shortly after completing his conquests and died at the age of 33 in 323 BC. With no living heir to the throne, the empire was divided up. Ptolemy Soter, one of Alexander's loyal lieutenants, ruled in Alexandria and completed construction of the library as Alexander had wished. There, the works of Aristotle and some of the sophists were preserved in their Arabic translations and studied by Egyptian and, later, Muslim scholars.

Although writings on rhetoric were preserved there, rhetoric was not a vital subject of study in Ptolemy's Egypt. Ptolemy and his successors ruled absolutely, and tolerated no advocacy of unapproved views. Centuries later, when North Africa was under Islamic control, Muslim scholars studied the texts in the Alexandria library, but most were not concerned with writings on rhetoric, since such skills were not recognized as important in their autocratic society. Instead, most Egyptian and Muslim scholars pursued the studies of mathematics, engineering, and architecture. One Muslim logician, Averroes, did address rhetoric in his work. Writing in the twelfth century, Averroes observed that truths revealed in the *Koran*, could be used to demonstrate other truths. Reflecting his own reading of Plato, he also discussed various types of audiences, the highest of which was devoted to "theoretical study," and the lowest of which was incapable of understanding theoretical books. He called this lowest class of audience the "rhetorical class" and suggested they should be taught by preachers and not allowed to read for themselves (Smith, 1998).

ROMAN RHETORIC

While Ptolemy and his successors ruled in Egypt, Rome grew powerful and conquered most of Mediterranean basin. Our image of Rome is that of an empire ruled absolutely by an emperor. However, during most of the period of successful Roman conquest, Rome was a republic (494 BC to 46 BC), with laws made by an Assembly whose members were elected by ordinary citizens, and a Senate, representing the aristocrats. Since decisions about laws in Rome were influenced by speeches in the Assembly and Senate, the subject of rhetoric was of practical interest. When Rome conquered Greece in 146 BC, Romans eagerly gathered and applied Greek knowledge and art. The works of Aristotle and the sophists were studied carefully, and the study and teaching of rhetoric were incorporated as central features in Roman education.

The Romans were not so much contributors of new ideas as they were experts at organization and discipline. Roman writings on rhetoric tended to bring together a variety of Greek ideas into an organized system. Cicero, the greatest of all Roman orators, was also a teacher and prolific scholar. In the 1st century B.C. he wrote seven books on the subject of rhetoric, drawing on a variety of Greek sources, but primarily relying on Aristotle. Cicero suggested that oratory has three practical objectives: to instruct, to please, and to win over, all of which were vital to functioning as a citizen in a Roman republic (Clarke, 1953).

In the first century A.D., when Rome was no longer a republic, Quintilian distinguished himself as an eminent Roman scholar, educator, and advocate. In his time rhetoric was still prominent in Roman life as a system of thinking, a central aspect of education, and as the practical art of advocacy, practiced before judges and rulers. Quintilian developed a detailed theory of rhetoric, organizing Aristotle's descriptions of the skills needed to speak effectively into to the well-defined list that came to be called the "five canons of rhetoric." At the center of his thought about rhetoric was the conviction that the "first essential" for a great orator was to be a good man (Clarke, 1953). Quintilian's ideal of the "good man speaking well" was Cicero, and Quintilian's students were required to memorize and recite Cicero's speeches. Quintilian found it necessary to look back to Cicero's time, the period of the Republic, to find great oratory. Empires are not safe places for great orators.

Rhetoric in Christian Europe

During the fourth and fifth centuries AD, Roman authority weakened and finally collapsed. As the Roman Empire disintegrated and migrating Germanic tribes populated what had been Roman provinces, the Roman Catholic Church became the primary keeper and purveyor of knowledge. In medieval Europe, the Church replaced secular authority as the central organizing and civilizing influence. Education outside the walls of Christian monasteries and a few royal palaces virtually ceased; much of classical knowledge, many classical documents, even literacy were largely lost to Western Europe.

In developing their view of rhetoric, medieval Christian scholars took their cue from Augustine of Hippo, the great Christian writer and preacher in the fourth century AD. Educated to be a rhetorician before his conversion to Christianity, Augustine struggled with the place of his rhetorical education in his life as a Christian. While retaining his appreciation for well-chosen words and elegant phrases, Augustine sought to guide Christians away from materialistic concerns and toward spiritual development of their relationship to God. His own view that important truths were received through divine inspiration resonated well with Plato's argument that truth is enduring and immutable, existing in an ideal, non-material form. So Augustine borrowed Plato's stance, suggesting that rhetoric could be used to help *impart* truths that were already known. He assigned rhetoric no part in the *pursuit of probable truth* for decision-making as Aristotle had advocated, but he did suggest that knowledge of rhetoric could be helpful in accurately interpreting scripture (Clarke, 1953).

In seeing rhetoric as a means to disseminate divinely inspired Truth about salvation, Augustine accorded rhetoric far greater respect than did Plato. Augustine wanted to improve Christian preaching in order to save more souls, and he recognized that rhetoric could be used for this purpose. He viewed Jesus Christ as the ultimate model for all speakers to emulate, and used his study of Jesus to further develop his view of rhetoric. He particularly noted how Jesus adapted his preaching to specific audiences (Smith, 1998). Augustine's understanding of rhetoric resulted in a brilliant blend of Plato's and Cicero's writings with scripture (Smith, 1998).

Although Augustine never used the term "communication," Peters (1999, p. 67) suggests that he was "in many ways a fountainhead of the concept of communication and a key figure in linguistic history." Augustine was an important early contributor to our understanding of how humans use signs and symbols to express ideas, and to our understanding of the concept of language.

THE CONTRIBUTION OF THE MOORS

During the period of Europe's decline, Islam took hold in the Middle East and in North Africa. As Muslims gained control in various areas, they eagerly acquired whatever knowledge existing cultures could offer. The ancient library at Alexandria was a cherished and well-used institution in Muslim culture, as were the works of ancient Persian scholars. Thus, the period we call the "Dark Ages" in Europe was an intellectual, artistic, economic, and military golden age for Islam. Muslim scholars not only acquired the ancient European knowledge deposited at Alexandria, but also added significant contributions of their own in philosophy, mathematics, and architecture.

Militant Muslims from North Africa known as Moors invaded Spain in 711 AD, and ruled much of Spain for almost seven centuries. During those centuries Europeans fought in periodic campaigns (crusades) to recover Spanish territory for Christianity. The city of Toledo, Spain served for many years as a Moorish administrative and cultural center, and the Moors established there a great library housing probably half a million books, most of which were copies of the works in the library at Alexandria, including Aristotle's and Plato's works. In 1085 AD, when Christian crusaders recaptured Toledo, the Moors retreated from the city leaving behind their library (Easton, 1966).

Recognizing that the Moors possessed considerable knowledge which Christian Europeans lacked, the new Bishop of Toledo ordered that the books in the library be preserved and translated into Latin for the benefit of Europe. Over the next four decades, Christian scholars, and a number of educated Jewish inhabitants of Toledo, labored to translate and copy the many works in the Toledo library. Copies of translated works were sent to Christian universities all over Europe. Among these works were several of Aristotle's writings, including the *Rhetoric*. This capturing of Muslim knowledge, and recapturing of Europe's ancient knowledge, helped stimulate Europe's Renaissance (Easton, 1966).

Christian scholars became interested in ancient Greek philosophical works, and some suggested that Aristotle's work on logic could be used to help explain theological issues. Aristotle's work, however, was viewed by most as highly suspect, since he had been a pagan, and these works came through the hands of the Muslims. As they struggled with the issue of whether and how to study non-Christian works, some Christian scholars were attracted by the ideas of Averroes, the Muslim philosopher who had argued that there are two kinds of knowledge, worldly and spiritual. Averroes suggested that while spiritual knowledge could come only through divine revelation, worldly knowledge could come from observation and reason. With this argument he had secured permission to study secular texts that might disagree with Islamic teaching. Such ideas, however, appeared to threaten Church authority in Christian Europe, and were officially disapproved (Easton, 1966). Only after Thomas Aquinas, the great French scholar and monk, showed that Aristotle's *Logic* could serve well to support Christian teaching did the Church permit more serious study of ancient Greek works. While Aquinas appreciated the potential value of Aristotle's *Logic*, he viewed rhetoric as a lesser study.

Among the ancient works studied, writings on rhetoric received relatively little attention from Christian scholars. When they did focus on rhetoric, many Christian scholars adhered to Augustine's basic view of rhetoric, although they also drew upon Cicero's and Quintilian's writings (Smith, 1998). Their contributions were to interpret Roman rules of rhetoric for their own time and circumstances rather than to develop new insights. They lived in an autocratic world where both spiritual and secular truths were decreed based on claims of divine authority. In such a world, rhetoric was relevant only for disseminating known truths and guiding the ignorant.

A few medieval scholars did attempt to advance the study of rhetoric. Alcuin of Notker, who served as chief scholar and teacher at Charlemagne's palace during the eighth century, produced enough new work to almost single-handedly constitute a mini-renaissance. One of his books, *New Rhetoric*, focused on finding effective arguments as well as on adapting speeches to specific audiences (Smith, 1998). A ninth century Irish scholar, John Scotus, focused on the use of rhetorical understanding to assist in interpreting texts (Smith, 1998). In developing the study of rhetoric for interpretive purposes, Scotus closely adhered to Augustine's notion that true authority comes from God through the church fathers. Thus, for Scotus, the purpose of rhetorical study was primarily to interpret the meanings of written messages.

Christians were not the only scholars in medieval Europe. The twelfth century Jewish philosopher, Maimonides, discussed rhetoric in his *Treatise on the Art of Logic,* and in his *Guide of the Perplexed*. Maimonides was highly impressed with Aristotle's *Logic,* and sought to introduce clear reason into theological discussions. Like Aquinas, however, he followed Plato's lead, viewing Aristotle's *Rhetoric* as useful primarily for teaching the truths to weak-minded audiences (Smith, 1998).

HUMANISM, THE RENAISSANCE, AND THE PRINTING PRESS

Humanism, an intellectual movement that began in Italy during the fifteenth century and spread throughout Europe, sought to fully understand, develop, and celebrate human nature and potential. Reacting against the spiritual constraints of medieval Christianity, humanists focused on earthly human achievements. These scholars made use of the works found in the Moors' library at Toledo. They sought out and translated whatever additional ancient Greek and Roman texts they could find, and they adopted the Greek ideal of the "universal man" who is learned and skilled in all things (Palmer, 1965). The efforts of the humanist scholars led to the Renaissance, to rediscovery of ancient Greek and Roman culture, and to a rebirth of Greek, Roman, and Muslim knowledge. Building upon the insights found in Muslim scientific and mathematical treatises, they profoundly advanced Western Europe's understanding of the physical world.

The Renaissance scholars' tendency to divide reality between the material and the immaterial and their penchant for dividing and categorizing subjects led to a fragmenting of the study of rhetoric. The French philosopher Peter Ramus placed the Aristotelian canons of invention and disposition (the mental efforts that create and organize the content of a message) within the domain of dialectic, which, he said, belonged to philosophy. The proper domain of rhetoric, he argued, included only style, memory, and delivery. This "Ramist" view of rhetoric was widely adopted in Renaissance Europe, and the study of rhetoric was thus narrowed to focus mainly on matters of language style and figures of speech, which were thought to be mainly ornamental. Influenced by Plato's writings, Ramus thought that ideas and human emotions were proper subjects for moral philosophers, and that rhetoric should focus on less weighty matters.

While Ramus and his followers narrowed the scope of rhetoric, other Renaissance scholars gave communication and language a central role in constructing the social world. They viewed literature as a means of philosophizing, because literature employed metaphor, irony, and rhetorical devises to construct meanings that included the specifics and the emotions of an event. Erasmus of Rotterdam, a 16th century Dutch humanist, argued that forms of expression were the means by which humans construct the institutions and ideas in which and by which they live. Giambattista Vico, an 18th century humanist argued that one cannot understand the world without understanding forms of communication, since the naming and labeling of experiences help to determine our perception of what the experience actually is (Pearce & Foss, 1990).

As Renaissance scholars thought and wrote about communication, one revolutionary technological advance profoundly altered human communication practices, and changed very structure of human society. Johann Gensfliesch, better known as Gutenberg, invented a printing press that made use of movable metal type. Adapted from a typical wine press of its day, this machine provided an efficient and inexpensive way to produce multiple copies of written texts, making it possible to produce thousands of documents and books. Prior to Gutenberg, written information had been available only to the clergy and the very rich; but the printing press made written information available to common people. In producing the first printed Bible in 1456, Gutenberg gave birth to mass communication (Schramm, 1973) as well as to the concept of mass production.

Among the effects print produced was that memory, the fourth of the five canons of rhetoric, became obsolete, and was largely ignored by rhetorical scholars thereafter. In the largely illiterate, oral society of Ancient Athens, information and ideas had to be stored in one's memory. In the literate world that was Europe after the invention of the printing press, information could be stored and readily retrieved from books. Memory was less important in a world where one could go to a library and look things up a book.

As Renaissance scholars abandoned the tradition of writing in Latin and began writing in their native languages of Italian, French, German, and English, and as their writings were printed and made widely available, an information revolution occurred in Europe. Reading became a useful skill for common people, who now had access to books and printed information. Writers addressed wide audiences, on all sorts of subjects. Because they could reach wide audiences across both time and distance, written words became more powerful than spoken words, and were seen as more important. The combination of the Renaissance and the printing press thus generated a new ideal for perfect communication, which was the exact opposite of Socrates' ancient ideal of perfect one-to one personal communication. This new ideal was a literary one, reflecting the new mass medium of print. The ideal literary message was regarded as one that could speak to all audiences, across time and space - - perfectly *impersonal*, communication. Given this ideal, rhetoric, which focused on *spoken* messages and on *specific* relationships between speaker, audience, and context, was deemed of lesser importance. The social world, the nature of human communication, and the study of communication were irreversibly changed.

THE ENLIGHTENMENT AND THE MODERN CONCEPT OF COMMUNICATION

The seventeenth century is called the "century of genius" because it was the age in which great geniuses such as Galileo, Isaac Newton, and Francis Bacon provided the fundamental insights that enabled science to become "modern." By the time Isaac Newton died (1727), scientific inquiry was a recognized major enterprise all over Europe and men of science were in constant touch with one another (Palmer, 1965). Inspired by the promise of scientific understanding, seventeenth and eighteenth century scholars boldly sought and confidently expected human "enlightenment" through science and reason. Given the extent to which they advanced human knowledge, "The Enlightenment" is a fitting label for their time.

Francis Bacon proposed a scientific approach in the study of human communication, suggesting scientific study of the gestures. Responding to Bacon's call, John Bulwer published *Chirologia* in 1644 addressing the nonverbal expression of thoughts and feelings (Pearce & Foss, 1990). Bulwer's work marks the beginning of scientific research on communication, and the beginning of the study of nonverbal communication.

John Locke, the great Enlightenment philosopher who gave Western Culture its ideals of individualism and democracy, also coined the term "communication" and gave it its modern meaning (Peters, 1999). In Book III of his *Essay on Human Understanding* Locke addressed the subject of language. Humans, he said, are "sociable," and language is "the great instrument, the Tye of Society" (Locke, 1690/1979, p. 402). He observed that words serve as signs by which the "thoughts of men's minds" are "conveyed to one another," and that speakers and listeners must share the same ideas about the meanings of signs for communication to serve its purpose (p. 406). According to Locke, all words and language should be made to serve the purpose of communication because without communication the "comfort and advantage of society" cannot be achieved (p. 403). In Locke's view communication provided the mechanism by which humans could co-exist and reap the benefits of society without compromising their individual sovereignty (Peters, 1999).

New Relevance for Rhetoric in England and the New World

Locke's ideas about individual rights and democratic government found their most persistent application in England and the United States. England's movement toward democracy had begun long before Locke's time, in 1215 AD, when King John was forced to sign the Magna Carta. Over time, the English monarchy gradually surrendered power first to English nobles, then also to English commoners. By the nineteenth century, England had become a *constitutional* monarchy in which the king shared authority with Parliament, where issues were debated and voted upon. This relatively democratic form of government in nineteenth century England provided fertile soil for a resurgence of rhetorical study, theory, and practice. Moreover, as the Industrial Revolution developed, bringing with it the growth of a strong middle and professional class, England was also fertile ground for broadening the study of human communication beyond the traditional boundaries of rhetoric.

During the late 18th and early 19th centuries three important English scholars, George Campbell, Hugh Blair, and Richard Whately, made significant new contributions to our understanding of rhetoric. Taken together, their works served to restore the study of rhetoric to its full Aristotelian scope, to blend rhetorical theory with psychology, logic, and aesthetics, and to move toward nesting rhetoric within the broader subject of human communication.

George Campbell added a strong psychological focus to our understanding of persuasion. In his book, *Philosophy of Rhetoric,* published in 1776, he suggested that rhetoric could be used to express ideas and create moods, as well as to argue rationally (Smith, 1998). Campbell believed the human psyche was composed of the understanding, the will, the affections, the memory, and the imagination, and that these elements could be combined by the speaker to create a unified emotional response in an audience (Smith, 1998). Campbell gave rhetoric a much broader purpose than the mere reporting of established truth. He included the canons of invention and disposition, restoring the rhetoric's original scope. He said the purposes of rhetoric were to "enlighten the understanding, to awaken the memory, to engage the imagination, to arouse the passions to influence the will to action or belief" (Smith, 1998).

Hugh Blair appreciated the artistic aspects as well as the persuasive aspects of rhetoric, and he taught and lectured on the subject throughout his adult life. The collection of forty-seven of his lectures on the subject published in 1783 as a book entitled *Lectures on Rhetoric and Belles Lettres,* was very widely read in both England and the United States. Blair preached that it was important to exercise good taste in speaking. He argued that ultimately, it is emotion, not reason, that drives human action, and he believed with Campbell that emotions aroused in an audience could be contagious (Smith, 1998).

Richard Whately, the Anglican archbishop of Saint Patrick's Cathedral in Dublin, Ireland, was particularly interested in the use of reason in persuasion. Reversing the position taken by Aquinas and Maimonides, and directly countering Plato, he viewed logic as a tool of rhetoric. In his book, *The Elements of Rhetoric,* first published in 1828, he utilized Aristotle's ideas to develop the modern study of argumentation (Smith, 1998), and his work on the theory of argument stood as the definitive for more than a century.

During the early 1800s the study of rhetoric was also a thriving enterprise in America. American universities included rhetoric as an important element in their curricula. Although early American rhetoricians were less influential than their English counterparts, they nevertheless made visible contributions to the study. John Witherspoon, one of the signers of the Declaration of Independence, was Professor of Rhetorical Studies at Princeton. In 1800, Witherspoon published *Lectures on Moral Philosophy and Eloquence,* the first complete treatise on rhetoric written in America. Before becoming President, John Quincy Adams served as Professor of Rhetoric and Oratory at Harvard. Adams' book, *Lectures on Rhetoric and Oratory,* was published in 1810. Noah Webster's son-in-law, Chauncey Goodrich, who was Professor of Rhetoric at Yale from 1817 to 1839, published a collection of analyses of British orators. Goodrich's work, titled *Select British Eloquence,* established the model followed by later historical studies of influential speakers, and continued to serve as an important rhetorical criticism text into the mid-twentieth century (Becker, 1989).

Elocution

Development of democracy opened the way for the study of rhetoric to more fully develop in England, France, and in the United States during the eighteenth century. At the same time, the Industrial Revolution and the rise of a middle class provided a new reason to broadening the study of human communication. One reason Hugh Blair's work on "belles lettres" became so popular in both England and the United States was that a large and growing number of people were moving from the peasant class into the new middle class. Middle class people needed to learn how to present themselves properly in polite company, and Blair's focus on proper taste in the use of language provided very helpful advice. Still, learning to present oneself properly was a significant task, and two important writers, Thomas Sheridan and Gilbert Austin provided an approach to address this need, advocating what they called "elocution."

Thomas Sheridan believed that by learning the principles of proper pronunciation, correct posture, and graceful movement, people could learn to present themselves well in polite society. In developing his ideas, he drew upon Locke's concept of communication, and on Bulwer's study of gestures, as well as on his experience as a professional actor. His book, *A Course of Lectures on Elocution* (1762) introduced the principles of elocution and offered the important new insight that the spoken word has significant properties which the written word does not have (Smith, 1998).

Gilbert Austin drew heavily upon the work of Sheridan and Blair, as well as upon classical rhetoric, to develop a detailed theory of elocution, which was published in his work, *A Treatise on Rhetorical Delivery*, in 1806 (Smith, 1998). Sheridan's and Austin's ideas form the basis of the study of elocution which flourished throughout the nineteenth and early twentieth centuries in England and the United States. Among their followers was Henry Ward, an English elocution teacher who claimed that by changing the way one spoke, he could change one's entire personality. Henry Ward served as the model for the fictional character Henry Higgins in *My Fair Lady*, and the plot of *My Fair Lady* is based upon Ward's ideas.

An important contribution of the elocutionists was their effort to treat the study of human communication as a science. Taking their cue from Bacon and Bulwer, they advocated basing conclusions about human expression on scientific observation. Francois Delsarte, a particularly influential French elocutionist, constructed complex theories, complete with careful diagrams and definitions to describe effective human expression. Inspired by Delsarte, and by Charles Darwin's book, *The Expression of Emotion in Man and Animals*, Moses True Brown, Professor of Oratory at Tufts College, asserted in 1886 that the study of communication had finally developed enough classified knowledge to become a recognized science (Cohen, 1994). Professor Brown's claim was somewhat premature, but the aspiration of the elocutionists to build a science of communication study may well have been a seed from which that science grew.

During the 1890s, Robert Fulton and Thomas Trueblood, Professors of Elocution and Oratory in Ohio and Michigan, both authored textbooks on elocution and public speaking, and edited collections of famous British and American orations (Cohen, 1994). Like Brown, Fulton and Trueblood claimed a scientific basis for their work and treated speaking as a practical skill, but their collections of famous speeches, which they placed in historical context, and in which they included biographies of the speakers, also gave their study a footing in the humanities.

In the late nineteenth century, elocution was widely taught throughout England and the United States. If one intended to function in the middle class as a merchant or as a professional, or as the spouse of a professional, one was generally expected to study with an elocution instructor, and to master the art of presenting oneself and one's ideas properly. In American colleges and universities, the study of rhetoric was mostly taught in English departments, and focused on effective *written* arguments and essays. Elocution instructors focused exclusively on *oral* communication. In some colleges elocution and oratory instructors were faculty members. In many places, however, these instructors were private teachers who located their enterprises near colleges. To be educated, one not only went to college; one also took lessons in elocution.

A Changing Academic World and the Birth of a New Discipline

For most of its 2500-year history, the study of communication focused primarily on public speaking, and was called rhetoric. Rhetoricians studied the Socratic concept of dialectic (pursuit of truth through an interactive logical process of asking and answering question), but they did not develop its interactive aspect into a broader view of communication. Rhetoric was consistently taught as one of the seven basic liberal arts throughout the medieval, Renaissance, and modern periods of European history. During the Renaissance, however, the study of rhetoric was limited to its "lesser" aspects of style and delivery, but written, literary communication was studied as a means of developing wisdom and of constructing society's institutions. At the end of the seventeenth century John Locke conceived and named our modern concept of communication, and in the context of a more democratic society nineteenth century scholars restored and added to the scope of rhetorical study. Elocutionists took up Locke's idea of communication as "minds meeting minds," but they did not pursue Socrates' ideal of personal communication: "souls intertwined in reciprocity" (Peters, 1999, p. 43). Interpersonal communication, mass communication, and communication as an ongoing, interactive process remained to be addressed in the twentieth century. At the dawn of the twentieth century the ancient study of rhetoric had survived and gained new relevance in democratic societies. The broader study of human communication, including scientific study, had been launched, but was fragmented and embryonic. It was not yet an academic discipline in the modern sense of the term.

The modern concept of professional academic disciplines, and the organization of universities into administrative units called "departments," did not develop until the late nineteenth century. Between 1860 and 1915 American colleges and universities experienced massive growth and major reorganization. Their growth was driven by rapid population growth, increased demand for higher education as people came to see education as a key to success in life, and government assumption of responsibility for providing education through the Land Grant Act of 1862. Reorganization of colleges was made necessary by their increased size, and was influenced by the development of new human sciences and an increase in specialization and professionalism among scholars.

In reorganizing to accommodate to the academic movement toward specialization into disciplines colleges and universities divided themselves into organizational units called "departments" that usually represented single academic disciplines. By the turn of the century, along with the older hard sciences (physics, chemistry, biology, astronomy), the newer social sciences had claimed disciplinary and departmental status, establishing departments of psychology, sociology, and anthropology. Scholars identified themselves as belonging to certain disciplines, forming professional associations and establishing peer-reviewed journals to report and discuss their findings

Some universities established departments of Rhetoric and Oratory, or Elocution; others created departments of English to study and teach the oral and written uses of language. English departments typically encompassed the study of literature, theater, written composition, rhetoric, and oral expression (public speaking or "oral English"). Thus, teachers

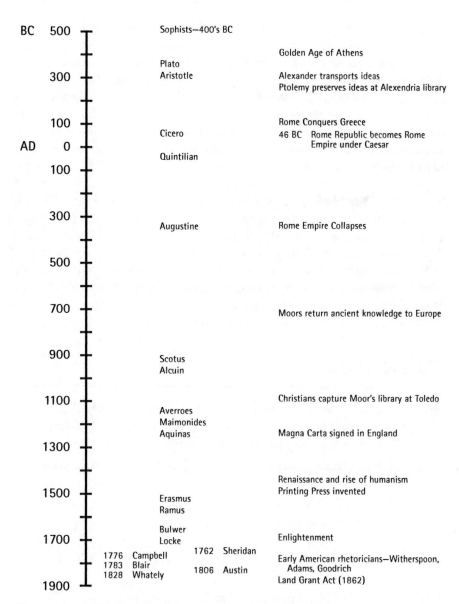

Figure 1   2400 Years of Communication Scholarship

of public speaking, elocution, and oratory were grouped with teachers of written composition and literature in departments of English.

The teachers of public speaking and rhetoric soon learned that English departments were not suitable homes for their work. Their focus and interests were on the *spoken word* and on the immediate effects of messages on specific audiences, whereas English departments focused on the *written word* and the study literature as fine art. As we shall see in Chapter 3, teachers of the spoken word came to view their field not as a subset of English, but as a distinct and separate study. In 1914 they began separating from English departments to form separate academic departments, and to define a distinct academic discipline they called Speech. They would build their twentieth-century discipline on the foundation of classical rhetoric and justify it for its practical relevance for citizenship in a democratic society. They would incorporate Locke's concept of communication as sharing of ideas and the elocutionists' pursuit of personal grace in interaction, and embrace scientific method to study communication as human behavior. And they would confront again the 2400-year old shadow Plato had cast over their study.

References

Becker, S. L. (1989). The rhetorical tradition. In S. S. King (Ed.), *Human communication as a field of study* (pp. 27-41). Albany, NY: State University of New York Press.

Clarke, M. L. (1953). *Rhetoric at Rome*. London: Cohen & West, Ltd.

Cohen, H. (1994). *The history of speech communication: The emergence of a discipline*. Annandale, VA: Speech Communication Association.

Easton, S. C. (1966). *The western heritage (4th ed.)*. New York: Holt, Rinehart, and Winston.

Howell, W. S. (1961). *Logic and rhetoric in England, 1500-1700*. New York: Russell & Russell.

Locke, J. (1979). An essay on human understanding (P. Nidditch, Ed.). Oxford, UK: Clarendon Press. (Original work published in 1690)

Palmer, R. R. & Colton, J. (1965). *A history of the modern world*. New York: Alfred. A. Knopf.

Pearce, W. D. & Foss, K. A. (1990). The historical context of communication as a science. In G. L. Dahnke & G. W. Clatterbuck (Eds.), *Human communication theory and research* (pp. 1-20). Belmont, California: Wadsworth.

Peters, J. D. (1999). *Speaking into the air: A history of the idea of communication.* Chicago: University of Chicago Press.

Schramm, W. (1973). *Men, messages and media: A look at human communication.* New York: Harper and Row.

Smith, C. (1998). *Rhetoric and human consciousness: A history.* Prospect Heights, IL: Waveland Press.

Chapter 3

Humanistic Study of Communication in the 20th Century

In Chapter 2 we traced the study of communication through 23 centuries, from the preservation of Aristotle's *Rhetoric* in the ancient library at Alexandria to the establishment of Departments of Speech at the dawn of the twentieth century. In Chapters 3 and 4 we will outline the modern study of communication, describing how the academic discipline of communication study evolved from 1910 to the present. Chapter 3 presents the ideas and contributions of rhetorical scholars to the discipline of Speech Communication during the first half of the twentieth century. Chapter 4 will focus on the development of the social science of communication over the second half of the century, and on the emergence of communication study as a mature academic discipline.

From Roman times to the mid-nineteenth century, rhetoric occupied a secure place in the academic world as one of the seven basic liberal arts around which higher education was organized. But the academic world changed dramatically in the late nineteenth century, and rhetorical scholars found themselves struggling to establish a new place for themselves in twentieth century universities. To appreciate their struggle, and to understand the strategic choices they made, we need to recall the circumstances in which they worked as the twentieth century began.

By the turn of the twentieth century American colleges and universities had experienced massive growth and were reorganizing themselves into departments that represented separate academic disciplines. Two criteria were typically applied in judging whether a study area should be considered an *academic discipline.* First, the content must represent a substantial and discrete subject area that is not covered by any other discipline. Second, the discipline must have a methodology of its own, that is, an accepted set of systematic methods for developing new knowledge about its subject. These criteria served well to identify specific sciences, but the study communication did not fit this narrow definition. Human communication was certainly a substantial subject area, but it was not discrete; the study of communication overlapped with studies of philosophy, logic, psychology, sociology, and history. Moreover, communication scholars employed a variety of methods in their work, depending on the aspect of communication they wished to address. Studies of rhetoric and oratory belonged among the humanities, but study of the physical act of speaking belonged to the physical sciences, and studies of group interaction were conducted using the methods of social science. Thus, there was considerable disagreement among communication scholars concerning research methods.

Since the study of communication could not be classified as a discrete academic discipline using early twentieth century criteria, colleges differed in where they placed it in their organizational structures. Some colleges created departments of oratory (or oratory and rhetoric, or elocution). Most placed studies of communication in departments of English.

In English departments, the written word was primary. The highest ideal of communication for English scholars was to produce and value literature as fine art, expressing universal truths for all audiences for all times. Recognizing that their scholarship and teaching were driven by different values from those of their English department colleagues , teachers of public speaking, elocutionists, and some rhetoricians began in 1910 to form their own professional associations, and to seek status as departments separate from English. As they worked to develop their modern academic discipline, to establish academic departments, and to build a solid curriculum of courses, early twentieth century communication scholars faced three daunting *disadvantages:* late arrival, lack of clear definition, and the lingering influence of Plato's Shadow. Let's examine these disadvantages more closely.

Late arrival: Despite the long history of communication study in Western Civilization, the study of communication was a latecomer as a modern academic discipline. Other newcomer disciplines, such as psychology, sociology, and anthropology had established their places in modern academia by 1900. Communication scholars and teachers established their first professional organization in 1910, formed their first national organization in 1914, and gradually acquired departmental status between 1915 and 1930. Thus, they faced the difficult task of carving out places for themselves in *already established* university structures.

Lack of clear definition: Their subject matter was not recognized as a discrete academic discipline. Its scope had not been clearly delineated. It overlapped with other subjects. It lacked an articulated methodology. It did not yet have an agreed-upon name. Rhetoric, public speaking, elocution, theater, debate, and the physical science of voice and speech all claimed inclusion.

Plato's Shadow: Finally, the questionable reputation given to rhetoric and rhetoricians by Plato, was still present (Bochner & Eisenberg, 1985). Like the sophists in ancient Greece, teachers of public speaking were purveyors of a practical art. Their efforts yielded good speeches, but the skills they taught could also be employed to make falsehoods appear true. The outcomes of their work were products (speeches) which, although they were clearly valuable when used to promote good outcomes, were not considered comparable to the discoveries of enduring truths which were the ideal outcomes of other academic efforts. In the twentieth century, as in ancient Athens, the rhetorician's work seemed tainted by doubts about its relationship to the pursuit of truth.

Along with these difficulties, communication scholars also possessed two powerful advantages as they sought to establish their discipline in modern academia. Their subject had practical value, and despite their "newcomer" status, they had deep roots as an academic tradition.

Practical value: Knowledge and skill in rhetoric (communication) had unquestionable practical value; the ability to speak effectively was an obvious aid to success in many professions, and a key to influential participation in civic affairs. This "practical art" fit perfectly with the educational mission of public universities—to provide economic opportunity to ordinary citizens by furnishing the knowledge and skills necessary to succeed. Since obvious practical value generated student demand for instruction, there was clearly a robust market for communication study (Cohen, 1994). This was the very same advantage that had kept the sophists in business despite Plato's condemnation, and the same essential value that had induced Aristotle to take up the study and teaching of rhetoric in ancient Athens.

Deep roots as an academic study: In seeking recognition as an academic discipline with departmental status, twentieth century communication scholars could draw upon a long history of communication scholarship and teaching. As we have seen, the systematic study of communication dated all the way back to ancient Greece, and instruction in rhetoric had been treated as an essential aspect of education for two thousand years. Classical concepts of rhetoric provided a strong foundation for their work. They could build upon a long and rich tradition of rhetorical scholarship, drawing upon the works of Plato, Aristotle, Cicero, Quintilian, Augustine, Scotus, Bulwer, Locke, Campbell, Blair, Whately, and many others. They may have been seen as newcomers in modern academia, but their scholarship sprang from deep and venerable roots.

Given the disadvantages they faced and the rich and complex history of their study, it is not surprising that early twentieth century communication scholars struggled to define their discipline, and differed among themselves in their responses to such fundamental issues as "What should be the scope of our study?" Or, "What principles should be considered foundational in building our scholarly method?" As communication scholars addressed these basic issues, one group sought to build its study on the foundation of classical rhetoric, and to focus on *speech as public address.* Another group sought to ally itself with the new social sciences of psychology and sociology, and to focus on the *human behavior of speaking* as its subject.

In December, 1915, a group of seventeen scholars met to address these issues, and to find common ground for a twentieth century discipline to address spoken communication. That meeting, many say, marked the beginning of the modern discipline of communication, and those scholars are dubbed its founders (Ewbank, 2001, p. 38). One challenging issue was the question of what this modern study of communication should be called. "Public Speaking", the label adopted by public speaking teachers when they formed their own professional association in 1910, was too narrow. "Rhetoric," the ancient label, excluded scholars who advocated a broader scope for their study. The term "speech", however, seemed to be an inclusive label that could be appropriately applied to both the rhetorical and the social scientific approaches, and that could also serve to designate the practical art of public speaking. So, the first label for the modern study of communication became "Speech." The Speech Association of America was formed as the national organization for professional academicians who studied communication. In colleges and universities where the new discipline was recognized, academic units labeled *Department of Speech*, or (when combined with scholars focusing on drama) *Department of Speech and Theater*, were established to conduct research and provide instruction in the practical art of human communication.

Rhetorical Scholarship and the Practical Art of Speech

The early architects of the rhetorical approach to communication study were a group of scholars at Cornell University that included James Winans, Everett Hunt, Herbert Wichelns and others (Leff & Procario, 1985). These scholars built their study and a coherent curriculum of courses on a foundation of classical rhetorical theory, primarily upon the work of Aristotle (Pearce, 1985). They adopted the sophists' goal of teaching *arete*, aiming to provide students with the communication skills they needed to function as effective citizens in both public and private life. They placed oratory, the public speech with political impact, at the center of their study, and labeled the skills they taught as "tools of a democracy" (Ewbank and Auer, 1941). In taking this approach, they capitalized on the two advantages we noted above; the practical value of their knowledge and their discipline's deep classical roots.

Focusing on rhetoric and oratory placed the study of speech in the humanist tradition, among the disciplines called humanities, which stressed appreciation of the unique qualities of human beings. Recall that humanism grew from a rediscovery of classical Greek and Roman thought during the Renaissance, and that classical rhetoric, philosophy, history and art were valued as methods of learning that contributed to human freedom in making enlightened choices. Early humanists regarded rhetoric as the medium through which human virtues could be communicated and achieved. Humanistic methods are interpretive, or critical in their approach to scholarship. Humanistic scholars are interested in gaining knowledge through studying individual cases; not in making generalizations across many individuals. From the humanist viewpoint, human beings are free to make conscious choices, and enlightened free will is the very essence of humanity.

In adopting a humanistic perspective and the sophists' ideal of *arete*, and in viewing their subject as an essential democratic tool, the Cornell scholars committed themselves to including both the content and the processes of speech making in their study. If inclusion of speech content in their subject matter meant that the study of speech over-lapped with other subjects, so be it. Grounding their study in Aristotle's *Rhetoric,* and in the works of Cicero and Quintilian, they asserted an ancient claim to the territory.

While acknowledging some shared subject matter with other dis-ciplines, the communication scholars advanced the case for treating rhetoric as a separate discipline from English through a series of articles published during the 1920s. The most influential of these articles was an essay by Herbert Wichelns (1925) in which he pointed out key dif-ferences between the rhetorical critic and the literary critic. He noted that while the literary critic's interest was in works that artistically spoke universal truths to all audiences in all times, the rhetorical critic's interest was in how effectively a specific speaker communicated with a *specific* audience, in a specific time, place, and context. He acknowl-edged the presence of aspects of poetry and literature in good rhetoric, but he clearly distinguished rhetoric from literature in terms of its focus and purpose. Noting how Aristotle distinguished rhetoric from logic on the one hand, and from poetic on the other, Winans, Wichelns, Hunt and others of the Cornell School adopted classical rhetorical concepts in general, and Aristotle's *Rhetoric* in particular, as the theoretical foun-dation of their study.

THE NEO-ARISTOTELIAN APPROACH

Over the next two decades communication scholars developed methodological details and standards, and adopted graduate and un-dergraduate curricula for the rhetorically based study of communica-tion. The methodology of rhetorical criticism based primarily upon Aristotle's concepts came to be called Neo-Aristotelian Criticism. In its mature form, it was fully described by Thonnsen and Baird in *Speech Criticism* (1948), which stood for more than a decade as the standard methodological text for rhetorical criticism. Applying these critical methods to important speakers and speeches in history, Neo-Aris-totelian scholars produced significant histories of public address in the United States and England.

Neo-Aristotelian rhetorical critics employed the classical treatises of Aristotle, Cicero, Qunitilian, and others, as well as nineteenth cen-tury English and American works on rhetoric, as theoretical bases for analyzing and evaluating specific speeches and speakers. The central questions these scholars sought to answer were drawn from Aristotle's definition of rhetoric, "the art of discovering all the available means of persuasion in a given situation." Assuming with Aristotle that a speech was an intentional effort to bring about a change in a specific audience, for a specific purpose, in a specific time, place, and context, they sought to understand how speakers adapted to all the specific conditions, and employed specific means of persuasion to achieve their purposes.

Neo-Aristotelian scholars rarely attempted to generalize about the nature of speech making when they drew conclusions; nor did they engage in literary or artistic analysis. Their efforts can be classified as specialized historical studies, since they viewed each speech as a unique event occurring in an historical context, and sought to develop better understanding of each speech as an historical event. They conducted systematic research, and added to our understanding of important speeches as historical events. Secondarily, their work contributed insights and models that have proved useful in developing public speaking instruction, and in guiding the thought of social scientists studying characteristics of the source, the message, and receivers in the communication process.

Rhetorical scholarship, with its focus on public speeches, became the most common approach to communication study in most American universities from about 1930 to about 1965. Implementing this approach, departments of Speech (or Speech Communication) developed curricula based on classical rhetorical theory, and aimed to develop students' practical communication skills. Their courses of instruction typically included classical, medieval, and modern rhetorical theory, methodology of rhetorical criticism, historical studies of English and American public address, public speaking, argumentation and debate, intercollegiate competition in debate, small group discussion, and persuasion.

In adopting classical rhetoric as the basis for their work, Neo-Aristotelian scholars unwittingly acquired some of its limitations and baggage. They thoughtfully distinguished their study of communication from the literary ideal of the universal message as fine art. They identified the civic value of rhetorical studies, but they did not seriously consider Socrates' ideal of intimate personal communication. The view of communication they adopted privileged public speeches, normally given by adult males who already possessed status in the community as the central objects of study. They adopted an explicitly Euro-centric code of rhetoric with emphasis on the ability to influence government decisions. Communication among women, children, and males who lacked status was hardly visible through the lens of rhetorical scholars.

We can appreciate their contributions to our study, but we must also recognize that their ideas imposed unfortunate limits. Their narrow scope excluded most people and most human communication.

A Broader Scope of Communication Study

Neo-Aristotelian scholars tended to view public speeches as single events, generally assuming a simple, straightforward cause-effect relationship between a speech and an outcome. By the 1950s, however, many rhetoricians recognized that this assumption was naãve. In the post-World War II world of propaganda machines, media politics, and influential social movements it became increasingly evident that persuasion was far more complex and more powerful in its effects than they could account for using the Neo-Aristotelian approach. As communication scholarship advanced to keep up with a changing, more complex world, the Neo-Aristotelian approach came more and more to be regarded as obsolete. Western culture-bound, and focused as it was on public speeches by privileged males, it offered few conceptual tools for understanding the effects or the politics of private interactions, or to appreciate the rhetorical styles of speakers who were women, minorities, or from other cultures. To understand and evaluate the communication of their times, communication scholars in the 1960s found it necessary to broaden their focus, find or generate new theories, and grow beyond the limits of Neo-Aristotelianism.

As communication scholars pursued other alternatives, Edwin Black's book, *Rhetorical Criticism: A Study of Method* (1965), signaled the end of Neo-Aristotelian ascendancy in rhetorical theory and criticism. Summarizing what many communication scholars were already thinking and doing, Black offered three reasons why rhetorical critics should reach beyond Neo-Aristotelianism to find other methods:

First, he pointed out that speeches represent only a tiny percentage of human communication, even a tiny percentage of rhetorical communication, and that speeches were hardly the most important aspect of human communication. Clearly, the scope of critical study needed to be vastly enlarged.

Second, he noted that if one is interested in determining whether a speech (or any other message) is effective, social science offers far better methods than rhetorical criticism. One can measure message effects by surveying the audience.

Finally, Black argued that effectiveness was not the only consideration in evaluating a speech. To drive home this point, he offered the example of the Coatesville Address, a commemorative speech given in 1912, at Coatesville, Pennsylvania to mark the anniversary of a brutal lynching of a African American man. The speaker, John J. Chapman, delivered his address because he believed the anniversary of that terrible event should not pass unremembered. Although he had advertised the speech in the newspaper and with posters, and rented the town hall for the occasion, only one person attended the Coatesville Address—a reporter on assignment for the local newspaper. The speech, though delivered to an audience of *one*, was eloquent and profoundly moving in its clear moral condemnation of racism and violence. Black reproduced the entire text of Chapman's speech in his book, and challenged rhetorical critics to say that this was not a valuable address. No one challenged Black's argument; effectiveness was clearly not an appropriate measure for this speech.

After 1965, publication of Neo-Aristotelian critical analyses dropped off sharply, replaced by alternative critical studies of messages and movements, and by social scientific studies of communication processes. Social scientific study focused more on interpersonal communication and on mass media messages than on speeches. Critical analyses focused more in interpreting the meaning and cultural impact of mass media messages. Communication scholars interested in practical application rather than theory development began focusing more on applying communication research in specific contexts such as organization management, small group problem solving, or political campaigns. The scope and emphasis of communication curricula and instruction broadened accordingly.

THE NEO-ARISTOTELIAN LEGACY

The Neo-Aristotelian era ended in the mid-1960s, but the scholarship it produced has by no means disappeared from the study of human communication. Neo-Aristotelian principles continue to influence our discipline in five ways.

1. Public speaking continues to be a very popular communication course in American colleges and universities. Skill in public speaking continues to be recognized as an important requisite for most professionals. The content of these courses is still based primarily on the rhetorical concepts distilled from Aristotle's *Rhetoric* by Neo-Aristotelian scholars.

2. Rhetorical criticism remains a significant area of scholarly activity. Contemporary critics rarely utilize direct applications

of Aristotle's theories, but they certainly employ Wichelns' focus on understanding the impact of a specific communicator, on a specific audience, in a specific place and context.

3. Argumentation and debate continue to thrive as both research and instructional activities.

4. The ancient sophists' ideal of *arete,* which views the purpose of education as helping students build the skills necessary for a useful public and private life, still guides decisions about communication curricula. Communication departments continue to design and offer undergraduate courses with clear practical value. Work by communication scholars in organizational, small group, health, and intercultural communication represents contemporary application of the ideal of *arete,* which Neo-Aristotelian scholars articulated for the twentieth century. In each of these areas of specialized communication study, useful application of communication research is a central focus.

5. Finally, the intellectual foundation for many contemporary theories of persuasion and social influence can be traced to Aristotelian concepts, definitions, and principles of rhetoric. Neo-Aristotelian scholars can justly be credited with bringing Aristotle's ideas about communication into the 20th century.

Rhetorical Theory Evolves

When American rhetoricians began seeking alternative methods for analyzing messages they found that brilliant scholars in other disciplines and other countries had developed insightful rhetorical theories, and provided new intellectual foundations for thought about communication. Among these were Kenneth Burke, Stephen Toulmin, Jurgen Habermas, Michael Foucault and Jean-Francois Lyotard.

Kenneth Burke, an American philosopher, provided a fundamentally new theory of persuasion, suggesting that it is achieved not by appealing to logic and emotion, but by a speaker achieving identity with an audience. Using theater as a metaphor to explain the process of persuasion, Burke identified five aspects of drama, which he labeled the *Dramatistic Pentad.* He employed these five aspects to develop a method of critical analysis that could be applied to determine *how* a speaker achieved *identity* with an audience, thus persuading them to the speaker's point of view (Nichols, 1963).

Steven Toulmin, an English philosopher of science, observed that daily decisions are made in response to informal arguments. He developed a new approach to the study of argumentation, which, instead of *prescribing* how people *should* argue, *described* how they *actually do* argue. The field of argumentation was revitalized in the early 1960s with publication of Toulmin's (1958) study of *The Uses of Argument*. Applying Toulmin's model of argument, scholars have dissected and insightfully analyzed a great variety of contemporary arguments. Toulmin's approach to argumentation was used in the ground-breaking text, *Decision by Debate* (Ehninger & Brockriede, 1963), and his ideas have been central to the American study of argumentation ever since.

Jurgen Habermas, the post-World War II German scholar who sought to build a set of critical methods that would prevent the rise of harmful totalitarian governments, asserted that people can and must liberate themselves by critically evaluating the content of their culture (Foss, Foss & Trapp, 1985; Smith, 1998). For Habermas, the fundamental purpose of rhetorical criticism was *liberation*, and the primary purpose for understanding persuasion was to defend oneself against it.

Michael Foucault observed that our perception of reality is organized through our language, and through culture-based rules of communication. Focusing on the spoken message as an event, Foucault pointed out the various ways spoken messages are limited by rules that control who can speak with authority and how messages must be structured and delivered to be credible. He showed how persons in power use rules of communication to control what is accepted as knowledge, and to keep others at the margins of society (Foss, Foss & Trapp, 1985; Smith, 1998).

Jean-Franciose Lyotard observed that in each society there appear to be "master narratives"—general explanations of the way things are, that these are accepted as general knowledge or systems of truth, and that they serve to limit and control people's lives. He suggested that in contemporary times, master narratives are breaking down and being replaced by what he called "local narratives," through which smaller communities establish varying systems of truth. Lyotard clearly articulated the postmodern epistemological stance, suggesting that pursuit of a single, certain truth for all is illusory, and that culturally imposed truth systems could be oppressive. He advocated recognizing that different "truths" are experienced differently, by different people, in different communities (Smith, 1998).

Communication scholars explored the ideas of these and other great scholars, applying them as theoretical bases and methodological tools to critically analyze messages. Communication scholars also developed *original methodological approaches* that were better suited than Aristotelian criticism for addressing important contemporary rhetorical issues. Below are some examples:

Observing that social change was often accomplished through social and political movements which were active over time, and which might include hundreds of speeches as well as many other symbolic acts, *Leland Griffin* (1952) developed and applied a method for rhetorically analyzing such movements. Over the next two decades, *movement studies* were applied both to historical movements, such as the abolition movement, and to contemporary movements, such as the Civil Rights Movement, or the campaign against the Vietnam War.

Lloyd Bitzer (1968) developed a systematic process for analyzing the situational context of a speech, providing a method for rhetorical critics to examine an important aspect of any speech that had not been adequately addressed in Aristotle's work. Observing that speeches occurred in a complex, emerging context, Bitzer pointed out how such factors as preceding events, timing, institutional conditions and rules, physical locations, and power relationships limit the speaker's options. His description of the *rhetorical situation* enabled rhetorical critics to better account for the impact of context in communication events.

Ernest Bormann (1972) observed that people use narratives to share their views about life; that is, they express and learn these outlooks by telling, and listening to, stories. Bormann labeled views about how life works "rhetorical visions," since the familiar themes contained in them create a shared, persuasive vision of reality that brings groups together. He developed an analytic method he called *fantasy theme analysis* to identify the persuasive messages embedded in the themes of narratives. Bormann's continued analysis of fantasy themes and rhetorical visions evolved into his theory of *symbolic convergence*, which powerfully demonstrates the value of bridging humanistic and social science perspectives.

Walter Fisher (1987) observed how extensively humans tell stories as ways of communicating and reasoning. In offering what he called the *narrative paradigm*, Fisher suggested that stories incorporate all the rationality of traditional argument, and evoke listeners' values as well (Littlejohn, 1999). Fisher's work provided the conceptual framework for a method of critically analyzing narratives by focusing on the events, characters, settings, and themes (Foss, 1989). The persuasive impact of a story could be evaluated by judging its coherence-whether it hangs together, and its fidelity, whether it rings true for the listener.

Hermeneutics and Postmodernism in Rhetorical Scholarship

In the late twentieth century, two important philosophical movements have significantly influenced humanistic communication scholarship: hermeneutics and postmodernism.

HERMENEUTICS

The term "hermeneutics" refers to the systematic analysis of messages (or texts) to explore their meaning. An underlying assumption of contemporary hermeneutic scholarship is that a single message can have many meanings, and that meanings vary with different receivers and different contexts. Hermeneutics is not a new form of research. As we observed in Chapter 2, during the fourth century A.D. Augustine combined hermeneutics with rhetorical theory to help interpret and explain Christian scripture to uneducated Christians. For centuries, Christian scholars in Europe and England employed hermeneutics to interpret their Bible (Smith, 1998). During the Renaissance hermeneutic scholars engaged extensively in efforts to interpret classical Greek and Roman texts.

Modern hermeneutic scholarship rests on philosophical foundations developed by European philosophers, such as Kant, Leibniz, and Dilthey. Kant reached the conclusion that matters of beauty and taste could not be judged by any external, objective criteria—that aesthetic judgments are subjective (Gadamer, 1960/1998). Leibniz developed the notion that human observation always occurs from some particular point of view—that there is no stance from which to observe universal truth. Dilthey argued that true hermeneutic understanding could be achieved only by dispensing with all dogma and rules (Gadamer, 1960/1998). These thinkers pointed out that while "truth" may exist in a general objective sense, the realities with which people actually live are "meanings." Meanings are perceived, interpreted, "truths," and these are always assigned by individuals and cultures, and are always influenced by context.

A significant twentieth-century contribution to hermeneutic understanding was provided by I. A. Richards (1936), who proposed a *new rhetoric* that would examine how people comprehend and misunderstand messages; not how they are persuaded through oratory. Richards sought to explain meaning. Drawing on John Locke's concept of communication, he proposed that although meaning is *conveyed through* words, which are imperfect symbols of the things they represent in the world, meaning *occurs* not in words themselves, but in peoples' thoughts. Most words can change meaning, depending on their *context*, which includes not just the phrases surrounding a word, but all the thoughts and experiences a person associates with the word (Ogden & Richards, 1946; Griffin, 1997). Richards asserted that people's thoughts and experiences influence the way they construct and interpret messages (Smith, 1998). His concern with meaning and misunderstanding helped broaden the study of communication beyond the narrow focus of speech making.

POSTMODERNISM

The term "postmodern" originated in the field of architecture. In the flurry of rebuilding and new building after World War II, the term "modern architecture" signified functional construction of buildings at minimal cost. Regarding "modern" buildings as drab and uninspiring, Philip Johnson, a leading American architect, began designing what he called "postmodern" buildings. Postmodern buildings were designed to reflect their local environments, and to inspire. Each was unique. Once expressed in architecture, postmodernism spread quickly through the American and European intellectual communities (Smith, 1998).

Like their namesakes in architecture, postmodernists in communication argued that societies damaged themselves by over-relying on science and technology. Influenced by the great German philosophers who developed hermeneutic theory, they were deeply suspicious of social science as an approach. Postmodernists argued that we live in a world fragmented into very different cultures, with differing systems of "truth," and that the claim of science to produce universal truth was bogus. Much of what passes for truth, they suggested, is defined by the culture in which one lives. The mechanism for building cultures is rhetoric, and the questions of who controls the rules of rhetoric, how, and to what end, are of primary importance. During the 1960s and 1970s, Michael Foucault convincingly showed that fundamental power in any culture is wielded through control of the rules of communication. Jean-Franciose Lyotard focused attention on the fact that our perception of reality is organized through our language, and that language (and therefore perceptions of reality) vary by culture (Smith, 1998). Lyotard explained that what we regard as "knowledge" always has a "sponsor," such as the church, a state, or a professional authority group. Sponsors, he pointed out, always have their own interests to serve (Lyotard, 1984).

Applying postmodern thought to the work of the rhetorical critic, Jacques Derrida, a French linguist, developed a method of criticism he called "deconstruction." With this method he sought to identify what a message excludes as well as includes, weakens as well as strengthens, forgets as well as remembers. Aware that every "yes" involves an infinite number of "no's", Derrida viewed discourse and scholarship as a kind of endless dance, with no final or certain answers at the end. He regarded rhetorical criticism as itself a very rhetorical act (Smith, 1998).

CONTEMPORARY RHETORICAL SCHOLARSHIP

Postmodern scholars today focus intensely on rhetoric. Their interest, however, is not in *whether* a message is effective, but in *what effect* the message produces. Although it is inaccurate to characterize these scholars as a group, most postmodernists would agree that they are concerned with the contents and outcomes of human discourse. Operating from the insight that all systems of knowledge are political, they critically evaluate messages and culture-based communication systems, often with the humanistic aim of helping to free individuals to more truly be themselves. Many focus their analytic efforts on interpreting meanings and outcomes of messages within their context, and assessing their merits accordingly. Many postmodernists are especially interested in how power is exercised through *control of the rules of rhetoric and language*. Most tend to view the Neo-Aristotelians' focus on specific arguments and persuasive techniques, and the social scientists' generalizations about specific communication behaviors, as naãve, superficial, culture bound, and oppressive. What postmodern communication scholars share with their early twentieth century counterparts is the recognition that communication affects virtually every aspect of human life, and that the abilities to understand and accomplish communication are indeed *practical arts*. What they share with the humanist tradition is the ideal of enabling individuals to function as free, choice-making creatures.

Some feminist communication scholars have found that postmodernism offers a useful intellectual platform for their work. Drawing on the ideas of Foucault, Lyotard, Derrida and others, they have analyzed messages, rules of communication, and language to identify the impact on women of a reality system created and controlled by men. Examining messages from the standpoint of a marginalized group in society, feminist rhetorical critics have shown how our language and communication conventions privilege a masculine perspective, and proposed ways to alter these imbalances (Foss, 1989; Smith, 1998). Feminist critics have also found it useful to employ Derrida's method to "deconstruct" messages, showing how they tend to "exclude, weaken, or not remember" women as a class. Feminist rhetorical theory attempts to show how a masculine value system has been privileged in most cultures, to give at least equal status to feminine values, and to help women become every bit as free in their choice-making as men.

Contemporary *humanistic* communication scholars interpret the "texts" of all forms of messages—speeches, poems, songs, videos, movies, advertising campaigns, conversations, even meeting interactions. Assuming that texts may have multiple meanings, these scholars aim to convince others to share their interpretation of how a text affects its audience. For this reason they are often referred to as interpretive scholars. Interpretive theorists have several purposes. In analyzing texts, they seek to expose their artistic appeal, to evaluate their cultural impact, to clarify the values and ideology embedded in the text, to develop theory, and perhaps to promote societal reform.

Summary

In this chapter we have seen how studies of rhetoric, oratory, elocution, and English in the early twentieth century provided a foundation for the twentieth-century rhetorical study of communication. To identify their modern discipline, communication scholars adopted the term "Speech," which gave primary attention to making speeches, but also named the act of speaking, allowing speeches to be studied employing the methods of the humanities, and the act speaking to be studied by social scientific methods. As decades passed the discipline's focus broadened and its name evolved, becoming Speech Communication, and later, simply Communication.

We traced the progress of the humanities-oriented scholars who defined themselves as rhetoricians and developed the Neo-Aristotelian approach to communication study. They studied classical rhetorical theories, developed methods to critically analyze messages based on classical theories, and delivered college courses in the practical arts of communication-public speaking, discussion, and debate. The influence of these early rhetorical scholars is still present in communication research and communication courses. As the limitations of Neo-Aristotelian scholarship became evident in the 1950s and 1960s, speech communication scholars sought and found valuable new rhetorical and communication theories articulated by scholars in other disciplines, and some speech communication scholars developed new methods of their own. In the second half of the twentieth century, hermeneutic and postmodern rhetorical theories and methods have guided rhetorical scholarship, as critics have sought to explain social changes, and to help liberate marginalized individuals and groups.

Our discussion of the evolution of rhetorical scholarship in this chapter represents only half of the twentieth story of communication study. We followed the trail of the Cornell group who took a rhetorical approach, placing their scholarship among the humanities and building instruction in the practical art of speaking. The social scientific study of communication, with roots reaching back to the seventeenth century works of Francis Bacon and John Bulwer, was represented in the discipline of speech as early as 1915. Scholars who, like Charles Woolbert, advocated pursuing the study of communication as a social science, were less influential than their rhetorical colleagues in the early twentieth century, but have since claimed a central role in the discipline. Their story appears in Chapter 4.

References

Bitzer, L. (1968). The rhetorical situation. *Philosophy and Rhetoric, 1*, 1-14.

Black, E. (1965). *Rhetorical criticism: A study in method*. New York: Macmillan.

Bochner, A. P. & Eisenberg, E. (1985). Legitimizing speech communication: An examination of coherence and cohesion in the development of the discipline. In T. W. Benson (Ed.), *Speech communication in the 20th century* (pp. 299-321). Carbondale and Edwardsville. IL: Southern Illinois University Press.

Bormann, E. (1972). Fantasy and rhetorical vision: the rhetorical criticism of social reality. *Quarterly Journal of Speech, 58*, 396-407.

Brock, L. E. & Scott, R. L. (Eds.). (1980). *Methods of rhetorical criticism: A twentieth century perspective* (2nd ed). Detroit: Wayne State University Press.

Cohen, H. (1994). *The history of speech communication: The emergence of a discipline, 1914-1945.* Annandale, VA: Speech Communication Association.

Ehninger, D. & Brockriede, W. (1963). *Decision by debate.* New York: Dodd, Mead & Co.

Ewbank, H. L. Jr. (2001). Henry Lee Ewbank, Sr.: Teacher of teachers of speech. In J. A. Kuypers & A. King (Eds.), *Twentieth-century roots of rhetorical studies* (pp. 31-70). Westport, CN: Praeger Publishers.

Ewbank, H. L. & Auer, J. J. (1941). *Discussion and debate: Tools of a democracy.* New York: Appleton-Century-Crofts.

Fisher, W (1987). *Human communication as narration: Toward a philosophy of reason, value, and action.* Columbia, SC: University of South Carolina Press.

Foss, S. (1989). *Rhetorical criticism: Exploration & practice.* Prospect Heights, IL: Waveland Press.

Foss, S. K., Foss, K. A. & Trapp, R. (1985). *Contemporary perspectives on rhetoric.* Prospect Heights, IL: Waveland Press.

Gadamer, H. G. (1998). *Truth and method* (2nd revised ed.) (J. Weinsheimer & D. G. Marshall, Trans.). New York: Continuum. (Original work published 1960)

Griffin, E. (1997). *A first look at communication theory* (3rd ed.). New York: McGraw-Hill.

Griffin, L. (1952, April). The rhetoric of historical movements. *Quarterly Journal of Speech, 38,* (2), 184-194.

Leff, M. C. & Procario, M. O. (1985). Rhetorical theory in speech communication. In T.W. Benson (Ed), *Speech communication in the 20th century* (pp. 3-27). Carbondale and Edwardsville: Southern Illinois University Press.

Littlejohn, S. W. (1999). *Theories of human communication* (6th ed.). Belmont, CA: Wadsworth.

Lyotard, Jean-Francois (1984). *The postmodern condition: A report on knowledge.* Minneapolis, MN: University of Minnesota Press.

Nichols, M. H. (1963). *Rhetoric and criticism.* Baton Rouge, LA: Louisiana State University Press.

Ogden, C. K., & Richards, I. A. (1946). *The meaning of meaning.* New York: Harcourt Brace & World.

Pearce, B. (1985). Scientific research methods in communication studies and their implications for theory and research. In T. W. Benson (Ed.), *Speech Communication in the 20th Century* (pp. 255-281). Carbondale and Edwardsville, IL: Southern Illinois University Press.

Richards, I. A. (1936). *The philosophy of rhetoric.* London: Oxford University.

Smith, C. R. (1998). *Rhetoric and human consciousness: A history.* Prospect Heights, IL: Waveland Press.

Thonnsen, L. & Baird, A. C. (1948). *Speech criticism.* New York: Ronald Press.

Toulmin, S. (1958). *The uses of argument.* Cambridge, England: Cambridge University Press.

Wichelns, H. A. (1925). The literary criticism of oratory. In A. M. Drummond (Ed), *Studies in rhetoric and public speaking in honor of James A Winans* (pp. 181-216). New York: Century.

Chapter 4

The Emerging Social Science of Communication Study

In advocating that the study of human communication be approached as a social science, Charles Woolbert represented a minority view among early twentieth century speech scholars. Still, Woolbert stuck to his position, publishing the first known experiment to explicitly test a theory of persuasion in 1920 (Becker, 1989). In the eighty years following his first experimental study of persuasion, Woolbert's view was gradually adopted by a majority of communication scholars. However, during the decades from the 1920s to the 1950s, when rhetoricians dominated the discipline of speech communication, it was primarily scholars in other disciplines concerned with human social behavior who were advancing the social scientific study of communication. As the scientific approach to communication study matured during the 1950s, 60s and 70s, it was embraced by speech communication scholars, and given a home in departments of speech communication and journalism.

In this chapter we will focus on the part of our intellectual heritage that comes from social science. Beginning with the roots of social scientific ideas and methods in the 19th century, we'll trace the historical development of the scientific study of communication throughout the twentieth century. Because of the breadth of our subject, this story has many plot lines, and it can be confusing. To comprehend the developments, it is important to understand the assumptions, methods, and purposes of social scientists. So, we begin the chapter with a brief explanation of social science, and how it differs from humanistic inquiry.

Social Science

As we have seen in Chapter 3, humanistic methods serve as analytic tools for interpreting the meaning and value of messages for their audiences. Humanistic scholars view humans as choice-making beings who experience individual realities that must be understood through interpretation. In contrast, social scientists assume there is one enduring reality, or universal truth of human experience, which can be discovered by systematically observing sensory data. Social scientists view human behavior not as a matter of free will, but governed by persistent rules or laws. They seek the best explanations for human behavior by systematically identifying those rules or laws, using scientific method. Social scientists are not interested in explaining unique events, individual behavior, or historical context; they are interested in drawing general conclusions that explain patterns of aggregate behavior (Babbie, 1986).

CHARACTERISTICS OF SOCIAL SCIENCE

Like the physical sciences, social science is grounded in *empiricism*, the view that sensory data, gathered through observation or experimentation, is the only reliable source of true knowledge. The empirical methods of social science are aimed at achieving *objectivity*. They are designed to protect against the inaccuracies and biases present in our informal observations and conclusions about human behavior. Although complete objectivity is an ideal that humans can only approximate, following accepted scientific methods minimizes error and bias, allowing researchers to agree that reality has been accurately observed.

Social scientists aim to be *descriptive*, not *prescriptive*. They concern themselves with accurately describing and explaining how or why things *are*; not with prescribing how things *should be*. Therefore, unlike humanistic scholars, social scientists do not address questions of *value*. They generally do not attempt to recommend improvements or solutions to social problems; only to understand them.

Scholars in the social sciences go through a three-step process as they seek to create knowledge. They ask questions, they observe, and they construct theories to answer their questions. In conducting their research, social scientists use both inductive and deductive methods. Quantitative scientists first construct theories, then test their theoretical hypotheses through observation (called the *deductive* method, reasoning from the whole to its parts). Qualitative researchers usually begin with observations, which may suggest questions, which in turn lead to developing a theory (called the *inductive* method, reasoning from parts to the whole). Wherever a researcher begins in the process, doing social scientific research involves the use of both inductive and deductive reasoning.

THE IMPORTANCE OF THEORY

Social scientists gain knowledge primarily through *theory building* and *theory testing*. Theories are explicit, logical explanations for how or why things occur in the world. Social scientists develop theories by reasoning logically about relationships among factors that contribute to a human phenomenon. Theories depict how these factors, or concepts, are logically related. From theory, researchers derive hypotheses, or specific predictions about how factors will relate to each other. They test their theories by doing empirical research to find whether those logical relationships exist in the real world, observing whether their theoretical hypotheses are supported by data. Researchers present their studies to other scientific scholars for review, and if they gain support, their studies are published, building a collective body of knowledge about human behavior. By developing and testing theories, researchers help organize and expand this pool of knowledge. Good theories accurately describe, explain or predict human phenomena with clarity, elegance and simplicity, filling in pieces to the puzzle of social life.

Quantitative and Qualitative Methods in Social Science

Social scientists use both *quantitative* and *qualitative* research methods. It is worthwhile understanding the differences between these two approaches to gaining knowledge, especially since one resembles humanistic scholarship. A simple way of distinguishing them is to say that quantitative researchers translate human behavior into *numerical terms* that enable them to draw conclusions about people in general. In contrast, qualitative research examines *words* and *meaning* in order to gain a deep understanding of people in context (Kazdin, 1998). Both methods rely on scientific principles.

QUANTITATIVE RESEARCH

Quantitative social scientists *quantify* their empirical data, or assign numbers to the observations, so that the results can be analyzed statistically. In order to work with numbers, quantitative researchers must operationalize theoretical concepts, or translate them into precise indicators (variables) that can be measured and statistically analyzed. This is a key step in the deductive method of theory testing. Statistical analyses are performed to test whether the hypothesized relationships among variables are supported by the data. Statistics are mathematical tools to help researchers decide if the results found in their studies are likely to occur across different groups or conditions in the world. Without statistics, scientists would have no means for generalizing their results beyond the sample of subjects that they observed.

Quantitative research is extremely valuable for coming up with *predictions* or *explanations* about human behavior. *Correlational studies* allow researchers to predict that certain conditions will occur together in our social world. Survey questionnaires are often used in correlational research. *Explanatory* research goes beyond prediction, and seeks to explain, or find causes for, phenomena. To isolate causes, researchers must conduct experiments, which test causal relationships by manipulating variables under controlled conditions. Experiments are the only way to determine causality, since they are designed to eliminate alternative explanations for research findings. Careful adherence to scientific method and proper statistical analysis allows us to have a high degree of confidence (usually about 95%) that study findings accurately reflect reality. For this reason, quantitative methods are useful not only for pure research, but also for evaluating programs and guiding policy decisions.

Quantitative methods are most appropriate when research questions are concerned with comparisons across different groups of people, when it is desirable to generalize results to a larger population, and when theoretical concepts can be effectively represented in numerical terms. Quantitative researchers narrow their focus of attention to examine only the factors they suspect are important contributors to a phenomenon, eliminating or ignoring all other factors. Consequently, their methods are not useful for capturing the complexity of life as it occurs holistically, in its natural surroundings.

QUALITATIVE RESEARCH

Qualitative researchers are concerned with accurately understanding and describing how people ascribe meaning to their experiences in everyday life. Like their quantitative colleagues, they seek knowledge in ways that are systematic, replicable, and cumulative (Kazdin, 1998; Williams, 1986). However, qualitative researchers ask questions about how people perceive, feel, and react to their situations in their natural surroundings; that is, *in context*-the very thing that quantitative researchers, in their efforts to generalize, work to eliminate. Qualitative researchers gain understanding through interpreting and elaborating, or making explicit, human conditions and events holistically as they occur in the world. Examples of qualitative research include in-depth interviews and oral histories, case studies, ethnography and conversation analysis. Sources of data include spoken or written words from interviews, diaries, letters, stories, photographs, films, or direct observation of participants in their natural environments.

In focusing on words and meanings rather than on numbers, and in relying on literary traditions such as narrative accounts that reveal human experience, qualitative researchers are similar to humanistic scholars in their research. However, their assumption that objective truth can be discovered through systematic observation and analysis places qualitative researchers in the category of social science. Like their quantitative colleagues, they use systematic methods of data collection, analyses, and ways to protect against bias that can influence the data. They accept the goals of science, but reject some of its procedures and assumptions, including the deductive method of starting with a theoretical explanation, then testing hypotheses, and translating meanings into numbers (Potter, 1996).

Qualitative approaches serve best when researchers seek to deeply comprehend highly complex events as they occur in the world, and when understanding the context in which events occur is important to understanding the events themselves. Qualitative research allows scholars to study concepts such as suffering, faith, hope and love. It can also be useful for investigating areas of human experience that are not well studied or to gain insights about a developing theory.

Summary: The Nature of Social Science

Social science assumes there is one, universal truth about human experience that can be discovered by using the scientific method to make empirical observations in the natural world. Scientific inquiry is designed to protect against the mistakes people tend to make in their informal questioning of why things are the way they are. Social scientists are not generally interested in explaining unique events, single cases, or individual behavior. Instead their goal is general conclusions that explain patterns of aggregate human behavior. They reach these conclusions by applying scientific methods of inquiry to systematically observe and account for human behavior. The scientific method consists of a systematic process of asking questions, making empirical observations, and developing theories supported by the observations. Social scientists use both deduction and induction in the processes of developing and testing theories. By testing theories, or logical explanations for social phenomena, social scientists add to the collective body of knowledge. Quantitative social science aims to predict or explain human behavior, using statistics to make inferences about an overall population that can be concluded from observed results in a sample of people. Qualitative social science aims to discover how people perceive, feel, and react in the context of situations, and focuses on interpreting meanings of texts. Both qualitative and quantitative research methods are important in social science.

With this basic understanding of social scientific approaches to scholarship, we can now describe how communication came to be studied by social scientists. This story is divided into three time periods: the birth of social science in the 19th century, the beginnings of scientific study of communication through 1940; and more recent history to the present.

Foundations of Social Science and Communication Study in the 19th Century

The roots of 20th social scientific methods lie in the 19th century beginnings of the disciplines of sociology and psychology. In the 1850s in France, August Comte advocated establishment of a single, comprehensive social science examining human society, which he called sociology. Convinced that social behavior was governed by natural laws that could be discovered through science, he believed that scientific methods should be used to study and improve society (Newman & Benz, 1998). He introduced the term positivism to refer to the use of modern scientific methods to study human society. Empirical methods of natural science, Comte reasoned, should be used to study human society. Unlike the unverifiable knowledge gained through metaphysics or theology, these scientific methods had the potential to yield "positive knowledge,"-knowledge that could be positively determined and confirmed through sensory data (Newman & Benz, 1998). Quantitative social scientists tend to be intellectual descendants of the *positivists*-followers of Comte's idea of applying the quantitative methods of measurement used in the physical sciences to the social sciences.

The social scientific study of psychology began with the work of Wilhelm Wundt during the 1880s in Germany. Like Comte, Wundt believed that human behavior was governed by natural laws. Wundt sought to discover these laws by applying the experimental methods used in the natural sciences. His methods were crude by today's standards. For example, he and his students played the roles of both experimenter and subject, and the number of subjects in his experiments was small-sometimes only one. Wundt and his German colleagues remained leaders in experimental psychology until the turn of the century.

American social scientists who study communication are also influenced by the ideas of two famous European social theorists of the 1800s. Charles Darwin's theory of evolution prompted the study of nonverbal communication in humans, and influenced the sociologists of the Chicago School, who viewed communication as a process of symbolic interaction. Sigmund Freud's psychoanalytic theory explained human behavior by examining the individual's unconscious mind. Although Freud used in-depth case studies (not scientific methods) to develop his theory, his ideas influenced Clark Hull's learning theory, which itself strongly influenced Carl Hovland's seminal persuasion research. Freud's psychoanalytic theory also influenced political scientist Harold Lasswell. The interactional view of communication (Watslavick, Beavin & Jackson, 1967), which examines human behavior as a function of *interpersonal* communication, was a reaction to Freud's *intrapersonal* view that behavior results from individual forces (Rogers, 1994). Darwin and Freud revolutionized 19th century ideas about human behavior and society. Their work had great impact on the early social sciences in America, and their ideas are still evident in some contemporary theories of communication.

Early Scientific Study of Communication: 1920s to 1940s

The early twentieth century in America was a period of vast, rapid and unrelenting social change. During this time, the nation experienced tremendous growth in population, industrialization, and urbanization. Social upheaval and technological advances in mass communication (radio and telephones) raised compelling issues for social scientists to investigate. Although not known as "communication research" at the time, communication was the subject of study in several fields, especially in politics, sociology, social psychology, speech and advertising. Let's look at some of these lines of research.

Politics and mass communication research. In the 1920s and 30s, between the two world wars, propaganda was of great concern in America. The power of mass political communication to shape national attitudes generated an abundance of propaganda research, led by Harold Lasswell's classic analysis of World War I propaganda techniques published in 1927. A political science scholar at the University of Chicago during the 1920s and 30s, Lasswell examined propaganda, the power of symbols, and public opinion. Lasswell's famous communication model, "who says what in which channel to whom with what effect?" (Lasswell, 1948) provided the unifying framework for much of the U.S. wartime research during World War II, and for later communication research (Delia, 1987; Schramm, 1997). Lasswell encouraged the development of *content analysis,* a qualitative research approach to systematically analyzing the content of texts. He deeply appreciated the complexity of social data and social life, so he was reluctant to rely on quantitative analysis, and always sought to Aget behind the data" (Schramm, 1997, p.34).

Propaganda became the focus of study for scholars across many disciplines, including political scientists, historians, social psychologists, journalists, speech and literary critics. Most researchers conducted interpretive studies using qualitative methods, primarily content analysis. They analyzed messages in newspapers, newsreels, high school history texts, movies, cartoons, political speeches, and magazine articles, to name a few. Some speech scholars began doing quantitative analyses of rhetorical devices in speeches in addition to interpretive analyses of speeches.

In addition to propaganda, public opinion became a central research focus during the 1930s. Walter Lippman, the famous progressivist journalist, was a central figure in public opinion research, in addition to Lasswell. Lippman believed that the press and public opinion should be studied by social scientists because mass media (i.e., the press) could mold citizens' knowledge and beliefs by reinforcing their stereotypic opinions, and this influence could be harmful to our democratic society. During the 1930s, public opinion research grew into a specialized quantitative field of study, influenced by research practices in political science, sociology and social psychology (Delia, 1987).

Psychology and Communication Research. The major thrust of psychology and experimentalism shifted to America after the outbreak of World War I in 1917 (Rogers, 1994). Social psychologists in America began conducting research on communication during World War I. Interest in social psychology quickly expanded, and by the end of the 1920s, social psychologists were conducting studies of persuasion and attitude change, group processes, the effects of movies on children, and interpersonal communication (Delia, 1987).

John B. Watson, a leading American psychologist, took the position that psychology must study only externally observable human behavior, since science can address only what can be objectively observed and measured. Human ideas and emotions, he said, occur inside the "black box" of each individual, and cannot be studied scientifically. Watson's approach, which came to be called *behaviorism,* was adopted by the majority of American social psychologists during the 1930s, 40s, and 50s.

Research on group dynamics after the first World War concerned questions about social norms in groups at the workplace, group facilitation, group leadership and decision making. Kurt Lewin, a German gestalt psychologist who also fled to America from Hitler's regime in the late 1930s, is known for his research on small group processes. Lewin was committed to applied research—he was a "practical theorist" who believed in testing theories by applying them to social problems in real life. His approach to studying human behavior combined humanistic and scientific perspectives. He avoided using statistical tests of significance because he was concerned that the individual case would be lost in the statistical analysis (Rogers, 1994). Lewin was the first to emphasize the cognitive approach in social psychology—the idea that an individual's thoughts both produce, and are the product of, communication. His field theory described the forces in an individual's social environment, including small groups, that influence individual behavior. Through his work on group dynamics, Lewin influenced communication research in the 1950s and 60s (Rogers, 1994; Delia, 1987).

Studying communication also became popular among educational psychologists from the 1920s to the 1940s. They investigated new technologies like radio in teaching, communication skills of instructors, readability of educational materials, listening, and instructional outcomes of communication.

Sociology and Communication Research. Much of social science as we now know it took shape at the University of Chicago during the 1920s and 30s. Researchers there were concerned with studying social issues and improving society, and were committed to using empirical research methods to "quantify" their findings. Their methods included observation and surveys to describe individuals' experiences within their social contexts. They viewed sociology as an applied, practical science oriented toward social action and reform.

George Herbert Mead, a professor at the University of Chicago, opposed Watson's behaviorism, arguing that unlike lower animals, humans are not "black boxes" because humans can communicate. People, he insisted, can tell scientists what they think and feel, and their reports can serve as valid data for study. Mead placed communication at the center of his study of human social processes. A *society*, he said, was a cluster of cooperative behaviors. Cooperation depended on communication, which depended on the use of symbols (Mead, 1934). Although Mead regarded himself a social psychologist, his ideas were more influential in the fields of sociology and communication. His description of how individuals construct their sense of themselves and society through language, or symbolic interaction, provided the foundation for a theoretical perspective known as *symbolic interactionism.* Symbolic interactionism has been widely adopted by both sociologists and communication scholars because it offers a broad overview of the role of communication in society (Littlejohn, 1978).

Led by the Chicago School in the 1920s, sociological research shifted toward quantitative approaches, and by the 1930s, the discipline of sociology was committed to empirical social science. The center of social research moved from Chicago to Columbia, where standardized methods of quantitative analysis suitable for examining national problems were greatly advancing (Delia, 1987). One of the Columbia professors was the sociologist Paul Lazarsfeld, who was most interested in the effects of mass communication, especially radio and films. Lazarsfeld had fled to America from Hitler's regime in 1932, and at Columbia, beginning in 1940, he directed a radio research institute that later became the Bureau of Applied Social Research. His chief research tool was the survey, and his work was the precursor to market research. Lazarsfeld's creativity as a researcher, his talent for bringing scholars together to work on projects, and his accomplishments in applied social research distinguished him as a leader in the study of mass communication (Delia, 1987; Schramm, 1997).

Quantitative methods, especially survey research methods and measurement of public opinion reached their peak in sociology after World War II. Meanwhile, the Chicago School focused on symbolic interaction. Their more qualitative approach provided a methodological foundation for Erving Goffman's (1959) dramaturgical analysis of self presentation and other everyday interpersonal interactions, of which communication is a central component.

Speech, Language, and Communication Research. Beginning with Charles Woolbert's work in 1919, scientific approaches were present in speech departments. But before the 1940s, social science research in speech departments was limited, probably because during that period their primary focus was on teaching speech as a practical art based on a rhetorical perspective. It is important to recognize, however, that social science research was advocated and conducted in speech communication throughout the twentieth century. Even James Winans, a leader of the Cornell School of rhetorical scholarship, called for social scientific study of communication as early as 1915 (Cohen, 1994).

At Yale University in the 1930s and 40s, Edward Sapir and his student Benjamin Lee Whorf, had developed their now famous hypothesis that the language people use shapes their perception, thought and culture. They reasoned that if a language is vague or limited, it would cause language users to also think in vague or limited ways. Alfred Korzybski, a Polish-American scholar, believed the solution for such language problems was to improve linguistic habits. He sought a non-Aristotelian, scientific basis for understanding the difference between words (symbols) and reality, and for comprehending the ways in which words influence the way we think. He laid out the principles of his theory of *general semantics* in 1933. These principles, which relate to methods for improving our habits of language use, still play a role in improving interpersonal communication skill.

Business and Communication Research. In the 1920s and 30s, Elton Mayo and his colleagues at Harvard Business School found a startling effect when studying the relationship between working conditions and production at the Hawthorne plant of Western Electric Company. Their experiments with changing lighting conditions showed that worker production increased when lighting was improved, when lighting was dimmed, and even when the factory lights were almost turned off! Noting that conducting each experiment required giving attention to the workers, Mayo speculated that friendly attention, rather than changes in lighting, caused the workers' morale and production to improve. He conducted groundbreaking experiments examining interpersonal communication and social organization among Hawthorne employees. The Hawthorne studies gave rise to the human relations school of management, which emphasizes employee participation and recognition as a means to improve morale and increase productivity. In this way, Mayo's research influenced future social science theory and research involving communication in organizations.

Advertising was another area that generated communication research. In the early 1900s, advertising was considered a positive agent for encouraging broad-based consumption and raising the standard of living. As national brands and national marketing mushroomed, research on advertising became commercially important. National advertising agencies began using researchers to conduct "scientific advertising" to discover what appealed to audiences in order to gain a competitive edge on the market. The commercialization of radio following World War I, prior to regulatory controls on broadcasting, also accelerated advertising research. Advertisers wanted data documenting the size and composition of their audiences, which led to research on communication and consumer behavior (Delia, 1987). Academics in communication departments looked down on conducting commercially- applied social science research, so much of what came to be known as "market research" migrated to schools of business.

Communication Research and World War II

World War II had a tremendous impact on the study of communication. The U.S. military considered communication vital in wartime efforts to influence the public and to train servicemen. The War Department needed to find effective ways to inform the American public about our goals in the war and about the need for food and gas rationing, and to motivate the public to support the war effort by growing victory gardens, and purchasing war bonds. The Department of the Army also needed to find ways to efficiently and effectively train personnel for military service (Rogers, 1997). The war brought together in Washington, D.C., four social scientists from different fields whom we now consider to be leaders in the scientific study of communication (Rogers, 1994; Schramm, 1997): political scientist Harold Lasswell, sociologist Paul

Lazarsfeld, social psychologist Kurt Lewin, and experimental psychologist Carl Hovland. We have already been introduced the first three; let's now consider Hovland.

Carl Hovland was an experimental psychologist at Yale who studied the effects of persuasion in the 1940s and 50s. Hovland had studied under Clark Hull, the behaviorist who developed learning theory based on the ideas of classical conditioning and Freudian theory. From learning theory, Hovland derived his "message learning approach," which assumed that since attitudes are learned, they can be changed through a learning process. In 1942, Hovland directed an experimental research program for the U.S. Department of War, working with Paul Lazarsfeld and famous social scientists (Rogers, 1994). His research team examined the effects of persuasive messages, source credibility, and fear appeals on soldiers' knowledge and attitudes (Hovland, Janis & Kelley, 1953). Hovland used the components of Shannon's linear model of communication—source, message, channel, and receiver—as variables in his many ingenious experiments on attitude change. His work is considered seminal in our field, and it strongly influenced later research in the areas of social influence and interpersonal communication.

One other key figure in the field of communication who was involved in wartime efforts was Wilbur Schramm. Schramm was, in Robert Gunderson's terms, the quintessential refugee in the study of communication. Educated in the humanities, he received his Ph.D. in English literature in 1932. His dissertation was an analysis of Longfellow=s epic poem, "Hiawatha." A prolific writer and a part-time journalist, Schramm was strongly influenced by Lazarsfeld's and Hovland's research. He worked for the federal government during World War II designing public information campaigns and studying their effects. He also helped draft speeches for Franklin Roosevelt's radio broadcasts, including his fireside chats (Rogers, 1994).

Schramm made major contributions to the academic field of communication. He was the first scholar to take an interdisciplinary perspective, integrating the work of social scientists in other disciplines who studied human communication. At a time when scholars in speech departments focused their attention primarily on speeches and speech making, the broader study of communication was attracting scholars from sociology, political science, psychology, even anthropology. Schramm brought these disciplines together into a new interdisciplinary field of academic work, which he called "communication study."

In 1943, during the war, Schramm organized the first interdisciplinary doctoral program in mass communication in the School of

Journalism at the University of Iowa. The curriculum included courses in psychology, sociology, and political science. Schramm's program was not the only program at the University of Iowa offering a degree in communication at that time. The Department of Speech and Dramatic Arts, Charles Woolbert's home department, had been the first academic department in the United States to study speech scientifically. Their work pioneered the study of interpersonal communication, and their students also were awarded degrees in communication.

The Growth of Communication Science after the War

In the decade following the second world war, communication research came into its own as a distinct field of study. The multidisciplinary war research by Lasswell, Lazarsfeld, Lewin and Hovland helped define the new field. Scholars were beginning to recognize the centrality of communication in political and public life, and these researchers looked to the systematic study of communication for solutions to the problems of democracy. Tremendous expansion in American higher education after the war was fueled by government grants and contracts for research, as we discussed in Chapter 3. Many colleges and state universities changed from teaching institutions to research-oriented universities, and emphasis shifted from teaching undergraduates to graduate education (Delia, 1987). New departments and programs formed to conduct communication research and to educate future communication scholars. In the 1950s, it was becoming increasingly clear that many of the important problems of this time were communication problems, and that studying these problems required insights and methods from several disciplines (Schramm, 1989). Doctoral programs and applied research institutes for the study of communication began to appear. Communication instruction and research institutes drew on theories and methods from sociology, psychology, anthropology and political science. Communication research methods included experimentation, survey research, and content analysis.

In the early 1950s social scientists studying communication adopted the term "communication research," and developed a common vocabulary of communication terms. They also agreed on a common conception of the basic communication process based on Lasswell's framework, "who says what, through which channels, to whom, with what effect," and on Shannon & Weaver's linear flow model of communication. Communication scholarship moved toward quantitative research and theory development that focused on the source, message, channel, receiver, and effects of communication (Delia, 1987).

After the war, Hovland and his colleagues continued their research on persuasion under the auspices of the Yale communication research program. Their experimental methods served for decades as models for other communication researchers, and experimental research became the preferred method among communication scientists, as it was among social psychologists. The accumulated work of the Yale program gave us a comprehensive understanding of persuasion, and is considered by many as "the largest single contribution to communication any man has made" (Rogers, 1994). Research on persuasion, also called social influence, continued to be very active during the 1950s and 60s.

Kurt Lewin's research on individuals in small groups continued through the 1950s. Since then, scholars in several disciplines have studied small group communication for the purpose of understanding and improving group processes and outcomes. The research has followed many paths, examining such topics as group member roles, group decision-making and problem solving, leadership, social networks in groups, phases of group development, conflict, and interaction among group members (Gouran, 1985). A few examples of small group research include: Robert Bales' analysis of group interactions showing that effective groups balance task activities and socioemotional activities; communication scholar Ernest Bormann's work revealing how tensions form among group members over time, and how sharing of "fantasy themes" creates solidarity among group members; and the research of Irving Janis, a Yale psychologist who had worked with Hovland, who developed the theory of *groupthink* to explain the conditions that cause a cohesive group to make foolish decisions (Janis, 1982). Although small group research has continued to contribute interesting and important findings since 1950, it has not been a major area of emphasis in communication study (Gouran, 1985; Littlejohn, 1999).

With the rapid expansion of graduate education in speech during the 1950s, speech communication researchers conducted studies of public speaking instruction, speech anxiety and stage fright, persuasion, group discussion, and learning from oral messages. By the 1960s, most of the researchers from other social science disciplines who came to communication had left the field, and a new generation of scholars took up the study of communication (Delia, 1987). A new brand of faculty with interests both in speech and in communication research (such as

David Berlo, and Gerald Miller) expanded the traditional areas of research to include more emphasis on persuasion, pyscholinguistics, group interaction, and speech education.

The major focus of communication research in the 1940s was the study of the effects of mass media, primarily radio and the press. Since its beginning, mass communication scholarship has been strongly shaped by concerns about the social impact of media, and by changing technology, historical events, and governmental or private interests (Brown, 1985; Delia, 1987). Prior to World War II, researchers like Lasswell proposed that mass media had strong, direct effects on audiences, who were thought to be uniformly and easily swayed by cleverly designed mass media messages. From the 1940s through 1960, psychologists and sociologists, including Paul Lazarsfeld, found that media had more limited, indirect effects, and that audience members' social relationships influenced how they responded to mass media messages. In the 50s and 60s, the advent of television greatly expanded the study of media effects research in the United States. By the 1970s, mass communication scholars recognized that a combination of factors influence the effects of media. They began to examine several intervening factors, including the agenda-setting role of news media, the influence of social networks and perceptions of popular support and among audiences, and the impact of repeated exposure to media. Researchers also focused more on the impact of public information campaigns, media influence on audience thoughts, attitudes and behavior, the flow of information in both directions between media sources and audiences, and the effects of communication events over time (Delia, 1987).

During the 1950s theory development and research in other disciplines also paved the way for the study of interpersonal communication. Psychiatrist Jurgen Ruesch and anthropologist Gregory Bateson (1951) co-authored a book on the role of interpersonal communication in mental illness which shed new light on the connection between interpersonal communication, relationships and personal well-being. Psychologist Fritz Heider (1958) began a program of research on attributions that remains a central concept in interpersonal theories today. Following in Darwin's footsteps, anthropologists Raymond Birdwhistell (1952) and Edward T. Hall (1959) observed and categorized individuals' body movements, gestures, postures and use of space during interactions. Their pioneering work laid the foundation for later work in nonverbal communication (Knapp, Miller & Fudge, 1994). In 1959 sociologist Erving Goffman published the first of many important books examining social behavior in daily life. Goffman (1959) viewed humans as actors engaged in performances that influenced, and were influenced by, their identities. He explored the relationship between social interaction and personal identity from a symbolic interactionist perspective.

By 1970, although public speaking remained the most widely enrolled course offered by communication departments, interpersonal communication had become a central focus for communication scholars. Social turmoil, the civil rights movement, and the Vietnam War in the 1960s led many young people and academics to reject the deceitful and manipulative aspects of mass media messages (both political and commercial), and the study of persuasion lost popularity. A new concern for personal development and integrity gave rise to encounter groups and sensitivity training, which featured face-to-face communication (Knapp, Miller & Fudge, 1994). Courses in interpersonal communication multiplied, and research in interpersonal communication became a major research area in U.S. colleges and universities. (This trend did not occur in Europe, Asia, or South America, where interpersonal communication is likely to be housed in disciplines other than communication, like psychology or sociology). In the 1970s and 80s, interpersonal communication theory expanded rapidly, with many important contributions from both interpretivist and scientific perspectives. Knapp and his colleagues (1994) have noted that the "bywords" of the 80s in communication departments were "relationships" and "messages." By the 80s and 90s, the study of interpersonal communication included a variety of both quantitative and qualitative approaches.

Integrating Speech and Communication Study

Wilbur Schramm's work helped integrate and shape the field of communication from 1948 through 1977 (Rogers, 1994). He organized academic programs to study communication at three major universities, trained the first generation of communication social scientists; and wrote groundbreaking textbooks for communication courses (Delia, 1987). He was the first person to hold the title "professor of communication." He envisioned an integrated social science of human communication in which existing departments of speech and journalism would be merged into one department that would study communication generically, including the study of interpersonal communication and media technologies (Schramm, 1997).

Schramm's vision and work fundamentally altered the field of communication study. During the 1960s, 70s and 80s, his approach was widely adopted in American colleges and universities. Its adoption took three forms. Some universities, often with the support of major private grant funding, formed schools of communication. These include the Annenberg Schools of Communication at the University of Southern California, and the University of Pennsylvania, the School of Communication at the University of Texas, and the School of Mass Communication at Stanford.

The most common manner in which Schramm's integrated view of communication was adopted was assimilation into existing departments of speech. Recognizing that significant new knowledge about communication could be developed using social science methods and an interdisciplinary perspective, speech and rhetoric scholars expanded their research efforts, their methods, and their course curricula. Seeking a useful marriage of rhetorical and social scientific scholarship, many changed their department names to "speech communication." During the 1960s and 70s, they added courses in interpersonal communication and mass communication. Major Midwestern universities, such as Wisconsin, Minnesota, and Indiana exemplified this approach.

Integrating contemporary communication scholars into traditional speech departments made sense intellectually; the subjects they studied belonged to the same family. Classical rhetorical theory articulated a clear set of discrete communication variables for social scientists to investigate. Early social science studies often focused on testing these variables. Aristotle's ideas on the use of emotional appeals and the role of ethos in persuasion are evident in a large portion of the work of Hovland's communication research program at Yale (Hovland, Janis & Kelly, 1953). Hovland's empirical approach to persuasion was even called "scientific rhetoric" (Maccoby, 1963). Later, Aristotle's dimensions of ethos (source credibility) were refined by the scientific work of David Berlo and James McCroskey (Becker, 1989). For the most part, these studies confirmed Aristotle's 2500-year old observations. Of course, scientific communication research also drew heavily upon modern social science theories. But as we have seen, the study of classical rhetoric shaped many of the ideas and research questions posed by scientific scholars, and in doing so helped build the understanding of human communication in the second half of the twentieth century.

The blending of rhetorical and social science scholarship was also reflected in the development of our professional associations.

The first major organization for teachers and scholars of rhetoric began in 1914, and soon changed its name to the Speech Association of America (SAA), then to the Speech Communication Association (SCA) in 1969, and in the late 1990s to the National Communication Association (NCA). In 1950, communication scholars who believed the SAA (now NCA) was not adequately concerned with communication problems in business and industry, or with social scientific approaches to studying communication, established the National Society for the Study of Communication, later known as the International Communication Association (ICA). Today, NCA embraces a full spectrum of communication scholarship, although it tends to emphasize historical, interpretive and critical approaches. The majority of its large membership identifies with the speech and rhetoric orientation to the discipline, although scientific researchers are welcomed. In contrast, ICA focuses more on quantitative social science approaches, and provides an intellectual home for scientific researchers in communication. There remains a large overlap in the membership and the subject areas of these two lead organizations in our field (Becker, 1989; Pearce, 1985).

Recent Trends in Communication Study

In the last twenty years, social scientific communication research has expanded and become more specialized. The use of both quantitative and qualitative approaches has increased (Rogers, 1994). Quantitative approaches have focused on studying cognitive structures and processes, interpersonal relationships, computer-mediated communication, and application of communication theories to behavioral, and public health problems. Among qualitative approaches, more studies have employed ethnographic and phenomenological methods. Using these methods researchers attempt to understand human interactions from the actors' own frames of reference, without preconceived expectations. There has also been more interest in interpretive research, particularly in feminist and cultural studies which aim to reveal power disparities among groups (Griffin, 1997). In general, since the 1980s, communication research and theory have focused on more specific aspects of communication, and on a broader range of communication activity.

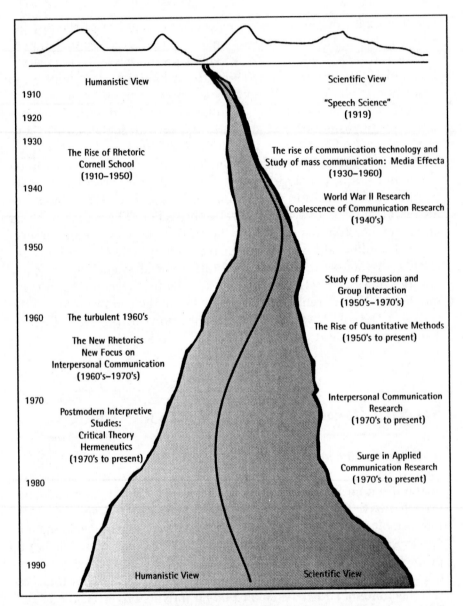

Figure 2   Communication Study in the 20th Century of influence in the flow of ideas (Adapted from Griffin (1997))

Summary

While the discipline of speech was dominated by Neo-Aristotelian rhetorical scholars, it was primarily scholars in related disciplines who made good on Woolbert's claims, developing of the social science of communication study. The emergence of mass media and social concerns in America from the 1930s to 1950s stimulated the growth of communication study by these social scientists. Mass media, war, and rapid technological change profoundly affected all human communication, and presented society with unprecedented problems and opportunities ripe for social research. Lasswell studied propaganda and public opinion, and Lazarsfeld was interested in the effects of the mass media on audiences. Lewin investigated the effects of social environments and group dynamics, and Hovland studied how mass media could be used persuasively. All four men applied their research to compelling social problems. Their work paved the way for broadening the scope of communication study to include the full range of human communication activity, expanding beyond persuasion to research in small group communication, interpersonal communication, mass communication, and many other sub-disciplines. Sometimes building on classical rhetorical concepts, and sometimes developing theories from other roots, social scientific communication scholars redefined the entire study of human communication. Their work has contributed a significant body of theoretical, methodological, and practical knowledge to our maturing discipline.

References

Babbie, E. (1986). *The practice of social research*. Belmont, CA: Wadsworth Publishing Co.

Becker, S. L. (1989). The rhetorical tradition. In S. S. King (Ed.), *Human communication as a field of study* (pp. 27-41). Albany, NY: State University of New York Press.

Birdwhistell, R. L. (1952). *Introduction to kinesics: An annotation system for analysis of body motion and gesture*. Washington, D.C.: Foreign Service Institute, U.S. Department of State/Ann Arbor, MI: University Microfilms.

Brown, W. R. (1985). Mass media and society: The development of critical perspectives. In T. W. Benson (Ed.), *Speech communication in the 20th century* (pp. 90-108). Carbondale and Edwardsville, IL: Southern Illinois University Press.

Cohen, H. (1994). *The History of Speech Communication: the emergence of a Discipline, 1914-1945*. Annandale: Speech Communication Association.

Delia, J. G. (1987). Communication research: A history. In C. R. Berger & S. H. Chaffee (Eds.), *Handbook of Communication Science* (pp. 20-98). Newbury Park CA: Sage.

Gouran, D. S. (1985). A paradigm of unfulfilled promise: A critical examination of the history of research on small groups in speech communication. In T. W. Benson (Ed.), *Speech communication in the 20th century* (pp. 90-108). Carbondale and Edwardsville, IL: Southern Illinois University Press.

Goffman, E. (1959). *Presentation of self in everyday life*. Garden City, NY: Doubleday & Co.

Griffin, E. (1997). *A first look at communication theory* (3rd ed). New York: McGraw-Hill.

Hall, E. T. (1959). *The silent language*. Garden City, NY: Doubleday.

Heider, F. (1958). *The psychology of interpersonal relations*. New York: Wiley.

Hovland, C. I., Janis, I. L., & Kelley, H. H. (1953). *Communication and persuasion*. New Haven, CT: Yale University Press.

Janis, I. (1982) *Victims of Groupthink*. Boston: Houghton-Mifflin.

Kazdin, A. E. (1998). *Research design in clinical psychology*. Boston, MA: Allyn and Bacon.

Knapp, M. L., Miller, G. R., & Fudge, K. (1994). Background and current trends in the study of interpersonal communication. In M. L. Knapp & G. R. Miller, *Handbook of Interpersonal Communication* (2nd ed.) (pp. 3-20). Thousand Oaks, CA: Sage.

Lasswell, H. (1948). The structure and function of communication in society. In L. Bryson (Ed.), *The communication of ideas* (pp. 37-51). New York: Institute for Religious Studies.

Littlejohn, S. W. (1978). *Theories of human communication* (1sr ed.). Columbus, Ohio: Charles E. Merrill Publishing Co.

Littlejohn, S. W. (1999). *Theories of human communication* (6th ed.). Belmont, CA: Wadsworth.

Maccoby. (1963). The new Ascientific@ rhetoric. In W. Schramm (Ed.), *The science of human communication: New directions and new findings in communication research.* New York: Basic Books.

Mead, G. H. (1934). *Mind, Self, and Society.* Chicago: University of Chicago Press.

Newman, I. & Benz, C. R. (1998). *Qualitative-quantitative research methodology: Exploring an interactive continuum.* Carbondale and Edwardsville, IL: Southern Illinois University Press.

Pearce, W. B. (1985). Scientific methods in communication studies and their implications for theory and research. In T. W. Benson (Ed.), *Speech communication in the 20th century* (pp. 255-281). Carbondale and Edwardsville, IL: Southern Illinois University Press.

Potter, W. J. (1996). *An analysis of thinking and research about qualitative methods.* Mahwah, NJ: Lawrence Erlbaum Associates.

Rogers, E. M. (1994). *A history of communication study: A biographical approach.* New York: The Free Press.

Ruesch, J. & Bateson, G. (1951). *Communication: The social matrix of psychiatry.* New York: Norton.

Schramm, W. (1989). Human communication as a field of behavioral science: Jack Hilgard and his committee. In S. S. King (Ed.), *Human communication as a field of study* (pp. 13-26). Albany, NY: State University of New York Press.

Schramm, W. (1997). (S.H. Chaffee & E. M. Rogers, Eds.) *The beginnings of communication study in America: A personal memoir.* Thousand Oaks, CA: Sage.

Watzlavick, P., Beavin, J., & Jackson, D.D. (1967). *Pragmatics of human communication: A study of interactional patterns, pathologies, and paradoxes.* New York: W. W. Norton & Co.

Williams, F. (1986). *Reasoning with statistics.* New York: Holt, Rinehart and Winston.

Chapter 5
Communication Study Today

Today the study of communication is made up of a rich blend of scholarly approaches examining a widening array of human behavior and concerns. Looking back across our long history helps us place our own work in the larger picture. Looking back, we can appreciate the deep and diverse roots of the ideas we use in our field, and see how the study of communication has evolved as the practice of communication has changed over time. In this closing chapter, we look at the study of communication today, address some enduring issues that confront scholars in our field, and consider how you fit into our community of scholars and practitioners.

At the beginning of the 21st century communication study is entering its 26th century as a thriving and growing enterprise. In the United States alone, some 1,500 colleges and universities include departments of communication or speech communication. The maturing social science of communication, the broadened, contemporary approaches to rhetoric, and the continually relevant focus on applied communication scholarship, have produced major growth in both enrollments and research. Undergraduate enrollment increased dramatically in the 1970s and 1980s, and has remained high. Between 1973 and 1992 the number of communication degrees awarded in the United States included 689, 917 BA's, 67,099 MA's, and 4,126 Ph.D's (National Center for Education Statistics, 1994). Undergraduates choose Communication as their major because it offers practical knowledge

Course[1]	Methods	Focus: Practical or Theoretical
1. Interpersonal Communication	social science	both
2. Group discussion (small group)	social science	practical
3. Communication Theory	social science	theoretical
4. Organizational Communication	social science	practical
5. Public Speaking	critical/social science	practical
6. Persuasion	social science/critical	both
7. Argumentation and Debate	critical	practical
8. Intercultural Communication	social science	both
9. Research methods	social science	theoretical
10. Rhetorical Criticism	critical	theoretical

[1] From Table 1, *Departments' Current, Expected, and Desired Course Offerings* (Wardrope, 1999, p. 257).

and skills that are useful in both professional and personal life. No other major offers communication's combination of applied skills, contemporary science, and cultural literacy-both a practical and a liberal education (Rogers, 1994). The fact that there are more than 30 scholarly journals in the communication field illustrates the strength and range of our academic discipline. The National Communication Association's list of 80 professions for which communication study is sound preparation illustrates the broad practical application of this field (Morreale & Vogl, 1998).

A recent list of the most popular communication courses in American colleges and universities (Wardrope, 1999, p. 257) illustrates the enduring influence of speech and rhetoric scholars, the emergence of social science in communication scholarship, and continuing interest in communication as a practical art. Below are the top ten courses from the list. We have added columns showing the primary methodological approach, and the practical or theoretical focus, of each course.

On the above list, the mixture of social science and critical scholarship, and practical and theoretical foci, is striking. Traditional speech communication courses compete with newer, social science based courses for top positions. Students are learning theory and research methods, but communication is still taught as a practical art. Communication teachers are still enacting the ancient sophists' instructional ideal of *arete*. They are providing knowledge and skills that are important for success in domestic and public life.

The Value of Different Approaches

Today, more and more researchers agree with Toulmin (1983) that the division between the scientific and humanistic scholarship is not rigid. In both forms of inquiry, investigators use interpretive processes (but in different ways) to make sense of empirical data (Potter, 1996). In both these forms, scholars ask questions, observe, and propose theoretical explanations. Furthermore, within social science, both qualitative and quantitative methods offer valuable ways of gaining knowledge, and combining methods can strengthen and enrich our understanding of the data (Flick, 1998; Newman & Benz, 1998). For example, to study how couples manage conflict, a researcher could use survey questionnaires (quantitative research), in-depth interviews (qualitative research), and an experiment (quantitative research). The point is that these different forms of scholarship are both important and often complementary in the pursuit of knowledge about human existence.

Challenges Facing Social Science

Social science faces difficulties that the physical sciences do not. It has a reputation of being a "soft science" because of its imprecise nature. Relative to the "hard" sciences such as physics and chemistry, which measure objects and events that do not have much individual variation, social science is considerably "messier." Why? First, studying human behavior is complex, since humans are individuals who think and act based on multiple factors. Humans behave with a great deal of variability, and may not act in conclusively predictable ways. Because of human variation, quantitative researchers need to observe a sample of people that is large enough to be assured that their experimental results are not due to unknown causes. For results to apply beyond just the individuals in the sample, these researchers also need to make sure that their sample is representative of the larger population of people from which it is taken.

Another reason why social science is naturally imprecise is that the phenomena social scientists study are abstract; they are not concrete and easily measurable. For quantitative researchers, measurements of abstract concepts depend on measurable indicators, which are never completely accurate or precise. For qualitative researchers, abstract concepts are necessary to explain complex events in relation to their equally complex contexts, yet complete explanations are never quite within reach. So the best that social scientists can do is use approximate indicators of theoretical concepts to discover partial (incomplete) predictions or explanations for human behavior. Because of these limitations, social science research is a never-ending effort in which researchers never quite reach their goal of complete understanding of social phenomena (Babbie, 1986).

Challenges Facing Humanist Scholars

Contemporary humanist scholars understand that the abstract concepts social scientists study, including ideas about what it means to be human, what constitutes a society, and what communication is, are themselves socially constructed, and that these are not universals, but belong to specific locations and groups, and change over time. For them the traditional scientific view that truth is constant and universal, and that the scholar's task is to discover and report truth no longer applies. The fundamental challenge faced by contemporary humanist scholars, therefore, is the problem of achieving agreement on what constitutes knowledge and what constitutes scholarship. In the contemporary world, where we understand the need to be "liberal" in accepting diverse systems of knowledge and radically differing cultures, what should we consider truth and what should pass for knowledge (Willard, 1996)? And, when a scholar critically analyzes a social or knowledge system for the purpose of liberating individuals from its harmful effects, how do we distinguish scholarship from politics?

Areas of Specialization in Communication Research

These challenges have tempered, but not deterred, communication scholarship. The sheer volume of new knowledge about human communication, and the enormous variety of its applications have led communication scholars to specialize in their research efforts. Some of the more common areas of specialization in communication research today are briefly described below.

Interpersonal Communication. The most basic unit of human interaction is the dyad-two people talking with one another. Interpersonal communication—the study of communication between two people, usually in face-to-face, private settings—has emerged over the past two decades as a central focus in communication research.

Relational Communication.   Relational communication is the study of interpersonal communication in close relationships, such as marriages, dating couples, or close friendships. Since relationships are constructed and enacted through communication (Duck, 1994), understanding how communication contributes to relationship development, maintenance, and disengagement is important, and of high interest to researchers today.

Small Group Communication.   The study of small group communication began in the 1930s by speech communication scholars who saw discussion and debate as essential skills for citizenship in a democracy. Today we study how small groups form and perform, and how groups and their members affect each other, through communication. An important new dimension of small group communication focuses on how computer mediated communication influences small group interactions.

Organizational Communication.   Organizations are social realities that are created, defined, and maintained through communication. Organizations are also contexts in which a great deal of human communication occurs. The study of organizational communication focuses on the relationship between communication and organization, exploring how organizations can become more efficient and effective, as well as psychologically healthier human habitats, through better communication.

Mass Communication.   Mass media (the internet, radio, television, film, periodicals) have important effects on audiences. The study of mass communication seeks to identify and evaluate those effects, and to identify ways mass media can be better employed to improve the quality of life. Mass media was the primary focus of early communication study, and continues to be a major area of quantitative communication research and extensive critical scholarship.

Political Communication.   In a democracy, politics is practiced through communication. How a politician communicates via television, newspapers, direct mail, or in person; how audiences react; and how well a politician listens; all affect elections. Political communication scholars analyze the outcomes of political communication through voter behavior, public opinion polls, and survey research.

Public Relations.   Public relations is not simply a matter of maintaining good relations with the press. It involves sending and seeking information between an organization and its environment. Every organization has many "publics," or groups of people with common interests.

As organizations seek to thrive in an increasingly complex and competitive environment, they need greater understanding of public relations processes. Public relations scholars seek to provide this understanding.

Intercultural Communication.   This research began in the early 1950s with Edward Hall's efforts to improve the abilities of US diplomats to communicate effectively with government officials representing countries with cultures that differ from ours. As the earth has become more like a "global village" through satellite and internet technology and increasingly interdependent economies, the study of how cultures differ in their communication rules and values, and how people can communicate effectively across cultures has grown steadily.

Family Communication.   Families are small groups made up of close relationships. Research in other disciplines such as psychology and sociology has shown that family life (composed largely of communication) powerfully influences family members' thoughts, feelings, and behavior. Communication scholars have become increasingly interested in family interactions, including those among parents, among children, and between parents and children in traditional and nontraditional families.

Health Communication.   Health communication is an important and fast-growing area of applied communication research that examines the relationship between communication and health, with an emphasis on communication in the health care setting. Health communication researchers recognize that communication behavior has health outcomes, and health conditions, in turn, affect communication. Theory and research examine health promotion campaigns, patient interactions with health care providers, interactions among health professionals, and communication among the ill or disabled.

Conflict Management.   Conflict management has been a part of communication study since the ancient Greeks invented the adversary system as a way to manage conflict among citizens. Since the 1970s, however, as the awareness of violence has increased, and the need for less adversarial processes to resolve conflicts has become increasingly evident in personal, organizational, and community contexts, the study of conflict management has become an important specialization in communication study.

Argumentation.   Grounded in the Aristotle's concept of *logos*, argumentation is the effort to persuade by appealing to reason (or giving reasons). Argumentation and debate have been important subjects in communication instruction since publication of Whately's *Elements*

Figure 3   Willy Elya, chief of the Hull tribe in Papua New Guinea, is online, showing his brand-new Web site at the International Tourism Fair in Berlin.

of Rhetoric in the 19th century. Refocused and re-energized by Toulmin's fresh approach, argumentation is a subject of both theoretical and practical research in Europe and the United States.

Nonverbal Communication.   For over 2,000 years, the study of communication focused mainly on the use of words-verbal communication. Since the 1950s, however, communication scholars have devoted increasing effort to examining the nonverbal codes through which humans communicate, and to observing how these are used in relation to verbal codes. Knowledge of nonverbal communication is important to understanding interpersonal relationships, since in face to face interactions, most of what is communicated is conveyed by nonverbal codes. Nonverbal research explores such topics as emotions, deception, attraction, distancing, intimacy, and accommodating to others.

Communication Technology.   The late 20th century produced an explosion of new communication technologies, such as the internet, satellite television, laptop and hand-held computers, and wireless phones. This trend will likely accelerate in the 21st century, with inventions that not only restructure the flow of information world wide, but dramatically change the ways individuals communicate about personal matters. Research exploring new possibilities, as well as measuring the expected and unexpected communication and relational effects of these new technologies is very much in demand.

Communication Study as Interdisciplinary Scholarship

Most of the specialized and applied areas of communication study listed above have interdisciplinary aspects. To study relational and family communication or conflict management, scholars must also study psychology and sociology. To study organizational communication, scholars must be familiar with current management theory and practice. To study the uses and effects of communication technology requires considerable technological knowledge. To study political communication, one must understand political science. As a result of this inseparable connection between the *process* and *content* of communication, many communication scholars today take an interdisciplinary approach in their work. They study and draw upon research in related fields, and often publish their communication research in the journals of related fields. We are not the "refugee scholars" Robert Gunderson described thirty years ago; we are "interdisciplinary" scholars, often combining our work in communication with one or more other disciplines to produce valuable new knowledge.

Enduring Issues Confronting our Field

Communication study is a firmly established enterprise today, but it is by no means a discipline without controversy. Enduring issues about which communication scholars and teachers have disagreed since Plato's time, continue to draw debate. These issues center around the following recurring questions:

1. What is communication? And what is the proper scope of communication study?

2. What are the primary purposes of communication study?

3. What methods are most appropriate for studying communication?

4. What is the value of communication study?

5. Where do we stand in our struggle with Plato's Shadow?

Let's take a closer look at the differing views on each of these questions.

1. The Nature of Communication and the Scope of Communication Study

Long ago, Aristotle defined "rhetoric" as the "art of discovering all the available means of persuasion in a given situation." For him, communication was all about persuasion. Communication was a conscious, strategic, purposive activity. Socrates and Plato, on the other hand, preferred to view communication as a cooperative inquiry in pursuit of Truth. For them, rhetoric was a purposive, strategic activity on the part of the teacher, though perhaps not for the student. Socrates' ideal for communication was an intimate, one-to-one interchange between two persons, in which the god-like beauty of each was revealed to the other. Since Socrates' time, every serious thinker about communication has struggled with the question of how best to define this subject. Twentieth century communication scholars continue to wrestle with important issues of definition. In doing so, they raise some difficult but very interesting questions, such as:

- Must communication occur between two or more persons in order to be considered communication? Or, should self-talk (*intrapersonal* communication) be considered communication?

- Does the *intention* of the communicator matter in determining whether to consider a behavior communication? Has communication occurred if a "receiver" perceives a message has been sent, even though the "sender" of the message did not intend to communicate?

- Does our subject include the *content of messages*, or are we concerned exclusively with the process of communication? In other words, is it the message sent that should be considered communication? Or, is it the *interaction* of the sender and receiver of the message?

- Is there such a thing as a *communication episode?* Or, is communication an *on-going system of multiple interactions*, with no identifiable boundaries?

- Where, if at all, should we place the *boundaries* that mark where the study of communication stops, and some other discipline begins?

Scholars' ongoing debates on these central questions help refine and mature our discipline.

2. THE PRIMARY PURPOSES OF COMMUNICATION STUDY

Throughout the social sciences, issues of purpose divide scholars into competing camps. Some insist that the scholar's purpose is to conduct "pure" research, generating new theory and knowledge. Their purpose is simply pursuit of truth; as social scientists, they seek to describe and explain human behavior rather than to prescribe solutions to human problems. For other scholars, the purpose of research is practical application; they seek to find and prescribe solutions to human problems through their scholarly work. This "pure research" versus "applied research" controversy is especially intense in the discipline of communication, where it mixes with the age-old problem of Plato's Shadow. Remember that it was the practical problem of individuals needing to develop skill in persuasion for political and economic gain to which the sophists responded by inventing the study of communication. It was the practical art of rhetoric that Plato criticized, but he allowed that something like a pure "science" which sought to understand the essential nature of human communication might be worth a philosopher's effort. Plato was absolutely correct in pointing out that rhetoric could be used to hide the truth as well as to present the truth.

NON SEQUITUR ©2000 Wiley Miller. Dist. By UNIVERSAL PRESS SYNDICATE. Reprinted with permission. All rights reserved.

Teachers of public speaking, focused as they are on helping students with the practical problem of presenting themselves and their subjects well rather than on discovering any new and universal truths, tend to be viewed as contemporary sophists in an academic world so influenced by Plato. So are consultants, who dispense communication advice to clients. Public relations specialists and press secretaries are seen as a bit glamorous on one hand, but ethically suspect on the other. And marketing and advertising are seen as economically productive, but morally questionable. Admittedly, teaching applied communication and doing applied communication research require laboring in Plato's Shadow. On the other hand, it is the need for practical skills that draws students to communication courses. And, it is the need for practical solutions to social problems that generates much of the grant funding for applied communication research, and the income for communication consultants.

Contemporary humanist scholars engage in deliberate efforts to improve the societies in which they work by critically evaluating their institutions, structures, and communication processes. Media critics and social scientists both study the effects of mass media messages. Their work serves to guide public policy in regulating mass media and to teach individuals how to insulate themselves from the harmful effects of television and film. When we consider the full range of communication study over its long history, we find that communication scholars have consistently attempted to conduct sound research and analysis with practical application for the individual and for society as a whole.

3. APPROPRIATE METHODS IN COMMUNICATION STUDY

Among communication scholars, debates about issues of definition, scope, and purpose are intertwined with issues of method. At the core of these debates are philosophical questions about the nature of truth and the nature of reality, and epistemological disputes about the nature of knowledge. Traditional social scientists assume that one true reality exists; that reality is knowable only through sensory data; and that certain knowledge can be achieved only through scientific methods. Therefore, traditional social scientists tend to disparage the methods of rhetorical and social critics. Many view postmodern methods as a corruption of genuine scholarship.

Postmodern theorists and critics begin with a fundamentally different philosophical stance. They assume that, while physical nature may exist as a single reality that is knowable through science, human cultures and societies are made up of social realities. Social realities, they insist, are not the same as the "hard reality" of physical nature, and cannot be understood or evaluated by applying methods borrowed from the physical sciences. There are many different social realities, each created and sustained by people through communication. Postmodernists argue that contemporary science, and the institutions and intellectual conventions that support it, are themselves social realities. Postmodern critics seek to evaluate the various social reality systems, to expose the ethical flaws in such systems, and to propose ways to improve them. The philosophical stance of postmodern scholars leads them to address fundamentally different questions than do social scientists, and to adopt correspondingly different methods.

Social scientists and postmodern critics both tend to treat the applied, practical art of rhetoric as useful, but of lesser value than scholarly research. They are comfortable with Plato's comparison of the practical art of rhetoric with "cookery." Perhaps even more than the general public, these scholars tend to be suspicious of communication practitioners, such as advertisers and public relations specialists, doubting their motives and their interest in discovering truth. Both groups of scholars tend to place the teacher of public speaking at the bottom of the status ladder among communication professionals.

The deep philosophical differences among communication scholars that drive the controversy over methods are understandable, given our rich history. In our view, this controversy is a healthy one, as long as scholars with different perspectives *keep communicating* with each other. Both rhetorical and social science perspectives are useful tools for gaining knowledge, and both can gain from each other. C. Arthur Van-Lear (1998) suggests that humanistic and scientific scholarship engage one another in a dialectical relationship in which each contributes to the advance of the other. Stephen Littlejohn points out that "Almost any program of research and theory building includes some aspects of both scientific and humanistic scholarship." "At times," he says, "the scientist is a humanist, using intuition, creativity, interpretation, and insight... In turn, at times the humanist must be scientific, seeking facts that enable experience to be understood" (Littlejohn, 1999, p.11). Marie Hochmuth Nichols, the distinguished rhetorician, stated that the "humanities without science are blind, but science without the humanities may be vicious" (Nichols, 1963, p. 18).

Clearly, both social scientific and humanistic approaches continue to occupy an important place within the discipline. Studying human communication calls for the use of both scientific and humanistic methods, and for scientists and humanists to learn from one another. Our wish is to see the advocates of competing approaches in communication study focus on ways their scholarship can be mutually supportive. Collaborating on a research question using a variety of methods could yield exciting insights not attainable from "inside the box" of each approach.

4. LIVING WITH PLATO'S SHADOW

Like any knowledge or skill, communication expertise can be used in the service of promoting good or falsehood. On the negative side, the more we know about how people process information, and how they are influenced by persuasive efforts, the more possible it is for unethical persons to mislead and control others. Today we live in an electronically mediated world where news is constantly managed and influenced by "spin masters." We are exposed to constant, highly sophisticated advertising. As a matter of self-defense, citizens must become genuinely cynical about messages, about practitioners who create messages, and about the theorists who inform those practitioners. "Sophistry," in the most pejorative sense of the term, abounds.

On the positive side, Aristotle's rationale for proceeding with the study and teaching of rhetoric seems more relevant today than ever. If ethical people fail to learn and skillfully use the best available communication principles and tools, unethical, self-serving manipulators will have their way, and control our minds, spirits, and material goods. Carl Hovland and his colleagues exemplified Aristotle's rationale when they developed persuasion theory for the purpose of countering Hitler's propaganda in World War II. Contemporary health communication researchers exemplify this rationale when they employ persuasion theories to develop and test anti-smoking media campaigns that counter the pervasive advertising of cigarette companies. Communication skills, communication technology, and communication theories are powerful tools. It is imperative today that good people master and use them.

Why, then, are communication scholars, teachers, and practitioners still doing battle with Plato's Shadow? It may be that Plato's characterization of the sophists and their work is so deeply rooted in western culture that the shadow is permanent. Our academic culture, with its powerful commitment to pure research—to the acquisition of knowledge for the sake of knowledge—tends to devalue matters of practical application. The ideology of modern science, which values development and testing of theories above all else, tends to diminish any study whose focus is interpretive or practical. And the dark side of communication endures, providing credible evidence to support the disparaging of communication study and practice. The shadow Plato cast over the study of communication will likely remain with us. It will require us to explain and defend our scholarly efforts. It may even prod us to be better scholars. What it will not do is prevent or diminish communication scholarship. Plato didn't win the argument against rhetoric in his own time, and his shadow pales against the mature study of communication in our time.

5. THE PRACTICAL VALUE OF COMMUNICATION STUDY

In Chapter 1, we introduced the idea of Plato's Shadow by telling the story of an argument one of the authors had with a fellow faculty member—a film instructor who disapproved of teaching students to debate, and who cited Plato to support his position. There is a sequel to that story, and the sequel is also worth telling. About three years after that discussion, the film instructor needed help on a matter of employment. His only hope of achieving tenure was to file and win a grievance case. But grievance cases are matters of argument, and he lacked the necessary skills. Nor could he afford to hire a lawyer to advocate his case. So, he turned to M.D., the debate coach, for help. Using the rhetorical skills the film instructor so sternly disdained, the debate coach advocated and won the instructor's grievance case, saving his livelihood. The film instructor was grateful, but he never became comfortable with the processes of argument and debate.

The point we wish to make in telling this story is that communication, including rhetorical communication, is so inherently central in human interaction that it is inescapable. Even Plato, in writing the *Gorgias*, found himself constructing arguments against rhetoric, and employing his beloved Socrates as a rhetorical device to effectively present his case. In any open and democratic society, the study and practice of human communication simply cannot be avoided. Its absolute practical value is enduring. Today the need for knowledge and skills in interpersonal, small group, organizational and intercultural communication is clearer than ever. Scholars are responding to the profound personal and social impacts of new communication technologies with research and new courses. It seems abundantly clear that the study of human communication must and will continue.

The value of maintaining a distinct academic domain of communication study also seems evident. Because communication is involved in virtually all human affairs, communication-focused research occurs in a broad variety of disciplines (Delia, 1987). When research about a subject is scattered across many disciplines, it is characterized by much unnecessary duplication and many unfortunate gaps. An important contribution of the discipline of communication study has been to pull together the fragments of communication knowledge developed in other disciplines into a more focused, integrated collection.

Communication Study and *You*

What is it that arouses your curiosity and makes you want to study communication? Is it the persuasive influence of television, radio, or the internet on children, consumers, or societal values? Is it the artistic impact of popular songs, music videos or movies on audiences, or the interpersonal problems that parents, lovers and friends encounter in their relationships? The subject of communication can be studied from dozens of perspectives, some of which you have read about in earlier chapters. The aspect of communication that you want to study, the questions you have about it, and your assumptions about how knowledge is acquired will guide your approach to studying communication, just as they do for communication scholars. After reading about these approaches, you may find that you tend to be more humanistic in your interests, while your classmate is more inclined to think scientifically about communication. You may want to pursue a career in public relations, while a fellow communication major wants to do research in health communication. That's fine. There's room in our discipline for many kinds of scholarship and practice. In fact, you have seen that we have a rich history of diversity upon which to draw.

We have outlined the story of communication study. Now we invite you to join us. You will be entering a thriving field of study that is both contemporary and ancient, and both theoretical and practical. Studying communication is fascinating and rewarding, but it is not easy. Human communication is marvelously complex, and communication concepts are often abstract. But we think the rewards are worth the effort. If you become a communication scholar, here is what we in the field ask of you, and what you can expect in return.

We ask you to:

- Understand the basic research methods used in communication study so that you can distinguish between sound communication advice and baseless speculation. Value good research and theory.

- Develop your theoretical knowledge of communication, and recognize how this knowledge can be applied for practical benefits.

- Develop a range of useful communication skills. Become proficient in the practical art of communication.
- Know and appreciate the historical and intellectual foundations of communication study. One should always be aware of the ground upon which one stands.
- Take your turn at boxing Plato's Shadow. There will no doubt be occasions when you will be required to explain and defend your chosen field. Plato was wise and right about many things, but he was wrong about the study and the practical art of communication.
- Keep up with the field after you graduate. New knowledge about communication is being developed every day. If you stop learning when you graduate, your knowledge will very soon be obsolete.

What you can expect in return (a shorter, but richer list):

- Deeper, fuller, and better human relationships.
- Greater awareness and acceptance of human differences.
- Greater success in virtually any vocation you choose.
- Greater ability to influence community and government affairs.
- And, if you become a professional communication scholar, an opportunity to generate new knowledge that can improve the quality of life for others.

To those who pursue it, the study of communication offers a unique perspective that spans across almost all types of human activity, and an exceptional opportunity to make a difference for the better in the world.

References

Babbie, E. (1986). *The practice of social research.* Belmont, CA: Wadsworth Publishing Co.

Delia, J. G. (1987). Communication research: A history. In C. R. Berger & S. H. Chaffee (Eds.), *Handbook of Communication Science* (pp. 20-98). Newbury Park CA: Sage.

Duck, S. (1994). *Meaningful relationships: talking, sense, and relating.* Thousand Oaks: Sage.

Flick, U. (1998). *An introduction to qualitative research*. Thousand Oaks, CA: Sage.

Littlejohn, S. W. (1999). *Theories of Human Communication* (6th ed.). Belmont, CA: Wadsworth Publishing Co.

Morreale, S. & Vogl, M. (1998). *Pathways to careers in communication*. Annandale, Virginia: National Communication Association.

National Center for Education Statistics of the U. S. Department of Education (1994). *Digest of education statistics*. Washington, D. C.: U. S. Department of Education.

Newman, I. & Benz, C. R. (1998). *Qualitative-quantitative research methodology: Exploring an interactive continuum*. Carbondale and Edwardsville, IL: Southern Illinois University Press.

Nichols, M. H. (1963). *Rhetoric and Criticism*. Baton Rouge, LA: Louisiana State University.

Potter, W. J. (1996). *An analysis of thinking and research about qualitative methods*. Mahwah, NJ: Lawrence Erlbaum Associates.

Rogers, E. M. (1994). *A history of communication study: A biographical approach*. New York: The Free Press.

Toulmin, S. (1983). The construal of reality: Criticism in modern and postmodern science. In W.J.T. Mitchell (Ed.), The Politics of Interpretation (pp. 99-117). Chicago: University of Chicago Press.

VanLear, C. A. (1998). Dialectic empiricism: Science and relationship metaphors. In B. M. Montgomery & L. A. Baxter (Eds.), *Dialectical approaches to studying personal relationships*. Mahwah, NJ: Lawrence Erlbaum.

Wardrope, W. J. (July, 1999). A curricular profile of U. S. communication departments. *Communication Education*,48(3), 256-258.

Willard, C. A. (1996). Liberalism and the problem of knowledge: A new rhetoric for modern democracy. Chicago: University of Chicago Press

Index